CLINICIAN'S
ILLUSTRATED
DICTIONARY OF
CARDIOLOGY

P – Z

CLINICIAN'S
ILLUSTRATED
DICTIONARY OF
CARDIOLOGY

compiled and edited by

Robert H Anderson BSc MD FRCPath

Paul J Oldershaw MD MRCP

Rex Dawson MBChB MRCP

with contributions from
Edward Rowland MB BS

The National Heart and Lung Institute
and the National Heart and Chest Hospitals,
Brompton Hospital, London, UK

P – Z

Presented as a service to cardiology
by Bayer UK Limited

science press

Acknowledgements

We would like to thank the following companies and individuals for permission to reproduce illustrations:
Figures 160, 161, 175, 176 and 192: Professor A.E. Becker, University of Amsterdam.
Figures 165 and 166: E. Braunwald, *Heart Disease: A Textbook of Cardiovascular Medicine* 2nd Edition, W.B. Saunders Company.
Figures 172a and 172b: Dr R. Underwood, National Heart and Lung Institute, London.
Figure 174: E. Sandoe and B. Sigurd, *Arrhythmia Diagnosis and Management* 1984, Fachmed AG.

This book represents the findings of the authors and is not necessarily the opinion of Bayer UK Limited.

Any product mentioned in this book should be used in accordance with the prescribing information prepared by the manufacturers. No claim or endorsement is made for any drug or compound presently under clinical investigation.

6 Lowther Road
London SW13 9ND, UK

British Library Cataloguing in Publication Data

Clinician's illustrated dictionary of cardiology

1. Medicine. Cardiology. Encyclopaedias
I. Anderson, Robert H. (Robert Henry), 1942-
616.1′2′0321

ISBN 1-870026-30-6

Design: Robin Dodd FCSD
Linework: Maurizia Merati
Printed in the UK by
Imago Publishing Ltd

P

P pulmonale

The electrocardiographic manifestations of right atrial enlargement are seen as a tall peaked P wave in lead II and a dominant tall positive deflection of the P wave in lead V1. These features, described as P pulmonale, are seen most commonly with long standing elevations of pressures in the right heart.

P wave

This wave is the electrocardiographic manifestation of atrial depolarization. Normally the wave results from depolarization of the sinus node, but the nodal discharge itself does not produce an electrical signal visible on the surface electrocardiogram. The normal P wave has a frontal axis of between 0°and 90°, is 80 – 120 ms broad and 0.1 – 0.3 mV in amplitude. The shape of the wave may be distorted by atrial enlargement, conduction defects within the atria, and when atrial depolarization results from impulse formation at a site other than the sinus node.

P_2

The abbreviation P_2 accounts for the pulmonary component of the second heart sound. This follows closely after the aortic component, the split between the two sounds varying with the phase of respiration. The delay is increased during inspiration while, during expiration, the delay is decreased. The intensity of the pulmonary component bears a close relationship to the pulmonary arterial pressure, and is accentuated by elevation of this pressure.

P-R interval

This interval on the surface electrocardiogram is measured between the onset of atrial depolarization (the P wave) and ventricular depolarization (the QRS complex). It is made up of the right atrial conduction time together with the conduction time through the atrioventricular node and His-Purkinje system. The normal range is 0.12 – 0.20 s, most of this interval being taken up by conduction through the atrioventricular node. The interval may be prolonged by abnormally slow conduction, usually at the level of the atrioventricular node.

Pacemakers

A pacemaker is an implantable device which contains a battery (usually driven by lithium iodide) and circuitry which produces pulses of short duration (0.5 ms) capable of stimulating the heart when delivered via an electrode which makes contact with the myocardium. Implantation of a pacemaker is necessary for the treatment of symptomatic bradycardia, or when the risk of bradycardia is sufficient to warrant prophylactic pacing. Typical indications are: complete heart block (either symptomatic or asymptomatic); advanced symptomatic second degree atrioventricular block; and symptomatic sinus nodal disease. The first permanent pacemaker was implanted in 1959. In these first pacemakers, the pacing lead was positioned epicardially. The superior performance of endocardial pacing has since been established, and the vast majority of permanent pacemakers are nowadays implanted via the transvenous route. Depending on the capacity of the battery and the frequency of stimulation, the generator may last between five and fifteen years. Regular follow-up is required to ensure satisfactory pacing and sensing function. Various modes of operation have been developed and many of the parameters of pacemaker function can be altered by non-invasive programming, using coded magnetic pulses transmitted from a programming magnet. The international classification of pacemaker codes and modes has recently been revised (Figure 154a). Less frequently, anti-tachycardia

Three-position pacemaker code

I. Chamber paced	II. Chamber sensed	III. Mode of response
V = Ventricle	V = Ventricle	I = Inhibited
A = Atrium	A = Atrium	T = Triggered
D = Atrium and ventricle	D = Atrium and ventricle	D = Atrial triggered and ventricular inhibited
	0 = None	0 = None

This code provides a shorthand description of pacemaker operation. The letters in the first two positions indicate the chamber(s) in which the pacemaker functions. The letter in the third position indicates the mode of operation of the pacemaker. Thus a pacemaker with a lead in the ventricle which does not sense ventricular activity is described as VOO; an atrial demand pacemaker is described as AAI. Dual, chamber pacemakers capable of sensing and pacing in both atrium and ventricle and in which the atrial sensing triggers ventricular output are described as DDD.

Figure 154a. Pacemaker.

pacemakers may be implanted which detect the onset of pathological tachycardia and pace competitively in order to terminate the arrhythmia. More recently, generators capable of delivering high energies for cardioversion of ventricular tachycardia or defibrillation from ventricular fibrillation have been introduced. Such devices are known as automatic implantable cardioverter/defibrillators.

Pacemakers can stimulate the heart at a *fixed rate* irrespective of the naturally occurring intrinsic rate, or a *demand pacemaker* may be used, which is capable of sensing the native rhythm and pacing the heart only when the sensed rate falls below a certain value. Recent advances in design have produced the *dual chamber pacemaker*, which is capable of synchronising atrial and ventricular activity (Figure 154b). Other variants are the *physiological pacemaker*, which is capable of increasing the

demand rate of the pacemaker in response to sensed physical activity, and the *ventricular demand pacemaker*. The latter is capable of sensing spontaneous

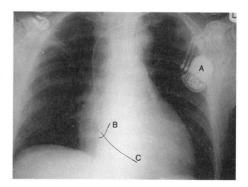

Figure 154b. Pacemaker. This chest x-ray shows a dual-chamber pacemaker in position. The pulse generator (A) is seen at the left pectoral region. From it, two pacing leads pass transvenously and end in the right atrium (B) and the right ventricle (C).

ventricular depolarization which then inhibits the output of the generator until the end of the preset or programmed demand interval.

Pace-mapping
This technique is one of pacing the heart at different sites to produce a surface electrocardiogram identical to that recorded during a spontaneous arrhythmia. The procedure enables localization of the site of origin of pathological tachycardias.

Pacing modalities
see *Pacemakers*

Paget's disease
(Sir James Paget, English surgeon and pathologist, 1814-1899)
This disease is also known as osteitis deformans. It is of unknown aetiology, but is characterized by excessive and disorganized resorption and formation of bone. It is said to occur in about 3% of all people over the age of 40 years, and is commoner in men than women. When severe, the disease produces heart failure as a consequence of the development of arteriovenous shunting subsequent to the excessive vascularity of the affected bones. Most patients with Paget's disease require no medication. In more severe cases, diphosphonates are used to reduce the excessive bony turnover. Calcitonin is sometimes recommended.

Palpation
This act is the art of feeling with the hand and fingers. It should always be part of the full cardiac clinical examination. The carotid, brachial, radial, femoral and foot pulses should be palpated to establish their presence or absence, the nature of their waveform, their timing relative to each other, and their rate and rhythm. Palpation of the praecordium provides information concerning the size of the heart and the character of its contraction. Palpation of the abdomen is necessary to exclude hepatic or splenic enlargement or the presence of ascites. See also *Cardiac impulse*

Palpitations
This abnormal feeling is an awareness of the beating of the heart. The perception may be a normal phenomenon when due to sinus tachycardia but is abnormal when due to an abnormal tachycardia.

Pancarditis
This term describes the involvement of all three layers of the heart (epicardium, myocardium and endocardium) in a disease process. Most frequently, it is used in relation to rheumatic disease.

Papillary muscles
The papillary muscles are the specific components of the ventricular myocardium which support the tendinous cords of the atrioventricular valves. The muscles are characteristically arranged within the two ventricles. Those supporting the mitral valve in the morphologically left ventricle are paired structures, each supporting the adjacent parts of the two leaflets of the valve at either end of the valvar commissure (Figure 155a). In contrast,

Figure 155a. Papillary muscles. The arrangement of the papillary muscles of the mitral valve.

the leaflets of the tricuspid valve within the morphologically right ventricle are supported by muscles of varying size. A small muscle, the medial papillary muscle (of Lancisi) supports the anteroseptal commissure. The prominent anterior papillary muscle either supports the anteroinferior commissure or inserts directly into the anterosuperior leaflet. Several smaller muscles support the inferior (mural) leaflet, while the septal leaflet typically has direct cordal attachments to the septum (Figure 155b).

Figure 155b. Papillary muscles. The arrangement of the papillary muscles of the tricuspid valve.

'Parachute' deformity of the mitral valve

Typically, the two leaflets of the mitral valve are supported by paired papillary muscles. When congenitally malformed, however, the two leaflets can be supported by a solitary muscle. In this situation, the muscle supporting the leaflets has been likened to a parachutist beneath the canopy of a parachute. The arrangement can be produced either by congenital absence of one muscle or by fusion of paired muscles into a solitary muscle mass.

Paradoxical embolism

This event is the blockage of a systemic artery by a thrombus which originated in a systemic vein and passed through a defect between the right and left sides of the heart. Usually, the clot passes through a patent oval foramen.

Paradoxical pulse
see *Pulsus paradoxus*

Parasystole

This ectopic rhythm is associated with entrance block and, therefore, is protected against premature discharge by the normal heart beat. The ectopic focus, in consequence, beats independently but it may produce excitation should the myocardium be excitable rather than refractory (Figure 156).

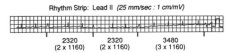

Rhythm Strip: Lead II *(25 mm/sec : 1 cm/mV)*

| 2320 | 2320 | 3480 |
| (2 x 1160) | (2 x 1160) | (3 x 1160) |

Figure 156. Parasystole. This rhythm strip shows ventricular extrasystoles with varying coupling interval to the preceding QRS complex. The interval between the parasystolic beats is always an exact multiple of the basic parasystolic interval (1160 milliseconds).

Paravalvar leak

This term describes the regurgitant flow of blood around the seating of a prosthetic heart valve rather than through the valve itself. The commonest cause of a paravalvar leak is bacterial endocarditis, but it may also be the consequence of inadequate suturing at the time of valvar implantation.

Paroxysmal atrial tachycardia

When previously used as a term to imply any supraventricular tachycardia in which a P wave preceded the QRS complex of a supraventricular beat, definition in this fashion did not allow the differentiation of atrial from atrioventricular junctional tachycardias. The term should be restricted, therefore, for description of those regular atrial tachycardias which arise from the atrium. The term ectopic atrial tachycardia is preferred. See also *Arrhythmia*.

Paroxysmal nocturnal dyspnoea
This cardinal symptom of raised pulmonary venous pressure is due to left ventricular disease, mitral regurgitation, or obstruction to normal filling of the left ventricle. The attacks follow a characteristic pattern. The patient wakes in the early hours of the morning with a sensation of suffocation, often associated with a dry cough, and, if the attack is severe, profuse sweating. The patient will often find symptomatic relief by changing from a recumbent to an upright posture, thereby reducing the hydrostatic pressure in the pulmonary venous and capillary beds. Often, the patient will describe a compulsion to get out of bed, walk to the window, throw it open and lean out, taking deep draughts of fresh air.

Partially anomalous pulmonary venous connexion
In the normal individual, all of the pulmonary veins are connected to the morphologically left atrium. Connexion of these veins to a site other than the left atrium is a well-recognized congenital malformation. This is most obvious when all the veins are anomalously connected *(totally anomalous connexion)*. Any of the individual veins, however, may have an anomalous connexion. The situation, therefore, where part of the venous return is to the left atrium with the remainder connected to a systemic site, is described as *partially anomalous connexion*. Anomalous connexion of a solitary vein usually has minor consequences, the degree of desaturation produced often escaping notice. Indeed, when searched for carefully, anomalous connexion of individual pulmonary veins is said to be found with some frequency in routine autopsies. Partially anomalous connexion can also be part and parcel of other lesions, such as the scimitar syndrome or the so-called sinus venosus interatrial communication. See also *Scimitar syndrome: Sinus venosus defect: Totally anomalous pulmonary venous connexion*

Partitioned right atrium
During development of the heart, the right atrium is derived in part from the atrial segment of the heart tube and, in part, from the venous sinus *(sinus venosus)*. In the early part of fetal life, extensive valvar structures separate these two components, serving also to direct oxygenated inferior caval venous blood across the oval foramen and into the left atrium. Normally, the valves regress to leave only the Eustachian and Thebesian valves but, in malformed hearts, they may persist or even become accentuated. They then divide the right atrium into two parts, giving a partitioned right atrium, often described as *cor triatriatum dexter*. See also *Eustachian valve: Spinnaker syndrome: Thebesian valve*

Patch, MacCallum's
(William George MacCallum, Canadian pathologist in U.S., 1874-1944)
This finding is one of the striking pathological features of hearts afflicted by acute rheumatic carditis. It is a roughened area of endocardium in the left atrium above the attachment of the mural (posterior) leaflet of the mitral valve. It was regarded by McCallum as part of a generalized endocardial involvement in the rheumatic process. It heals by becoming avascular fibrous tissue and may then calcify. Similar lesions may be seen in the right atrium, particularly within the oval fossa, but ventricular endocarditis is limited to extensions from valvar involvement.

Patency of arterial duct (ductus arteriosus)

The arterial duct is an integral part of the fetal circulation, conveying the deoxygenated blood from the right ventricle directly to the descending aorta so as to bypass the pulmonary circulation. Normally, the duct closes at birth due, in part, to a drop in levels of circulatory prostaglandins. Anatomically, it is converted to a ligament within the first six weeks of life. The changes preparing the duct for closure, however, occur during the last two months of intrauterine life. Babies born prematurely, therefore, have immature ducts which do not immediately close, but undergo obliteration as the neonate becomes more mature. This situation is to be distinguished from persistent patency of the duct, when the channel fails to close in a full-term neonate. There is evidence to show that the persistently patent duct has an abnormal histological structure which underscores the failure of its physiologic closure. Be that as it may, the consequence of failure of closure is a communication between the circulations at the level of the arterial trunks.

Aetiology. Persistent patency of the duct is one of the commonest congenital lesions, being particularly frequent in populations living at high altitude. It is also one of the lesions produced by the rubella virus. A patent duct may be expected when one arterial trunk is atretic or severely stenotic.

Diagnosis. The time of presentation depends on the size of the duct. When large, presentation is usually in the second month of life when the normal fall in pulmonary arterial pressure exacerbates the left-to-right shunt. Patency of the duct in premature infants, however, in whom pulmonary vascular resistance is usually low, typically produces overt signs of heart failure in the first week of life. Many patients with a patent duct, nonetheless, are not diagnosed until a murmur is heard at school medical examinations or even later. The murmur is continuous and maximal in the second left intercostal space at the left sternal edge. Diagnosis nowadays is confirmed by cross-sectional echocardiography.

Treatment. Surgery for closure of the persistently patent arterial duct should be accomplished with complete success and virtually zero mortality. In premature infants, however, it is usual first to attempt therapeutic closure using an inhibitor of prostaglandin such as indomethacin. Surgery should be performed if therapeutic manipulation is not immediately successful, but carries higher risks in the premature infant. In older patients, there is an increasing tendency towards closure by means of an umbrella device inserted by means of cardiac catheterization, thus avoiding a thoracotomy.

Pectus carinatum

The word 'carina' is Latin for the keel of a ship. The term 'pectus carinatum', describes a congenital thoracic deformity in which there is prominence of the upper sternum and adjacent costal cartilages with marked backward sloping of the ribs. It is known, less exotically but equally descriptively, as *'pigeon chest'*. Kyphoscoliosis is commonly associated. A pigeon chest may be found in patients with Marfan's syndrome and in homocystinuria.

Pectus excavatum

This term is used for description of the so-called funnel chest, in which there is posterior displacement of the lower sternum. The deformity may displace the heart into the left chest, producing prominence of the pulmonary trunk and apparent enlargement of the heart on chest x-ray. A funnel chest may be found in Marfan's syndrome, Ehlers-Danlos syndrome, and in patients with the straight back syndrome.

PEEP
see *Positive end expiratory pressure*

Pentaerythritol
see *Nitrates and nitrites*

Pentaerythritol tetranitrate
see *Nitrates and nitrites*

Pentalogy of Cantrell
The severest form of congenital malposition of the heart is when the heart is located outside the chest (ectopia cordis). Most commonly, the ectopic heart is displaced into the abdomen, and most patients with this abnormality are unified by having five features in common, namely, a midline deficiency of the abdominal wall, a defect of the lower part of the sternum, a deficiency of the pericardial sac, a deficiency of the diaphragm and an intracardiac congenital lesion. The association of these lesions was first noted by Cantrell and his colleagues in 1958, and the pentalogy is now known eponymously for him.

PEP
Pre-ejection period. See *Systolic time intervals*

Percussion of the heart
This feature of the clinical examination is rarely used in contemporary clinical practice. It involves tapping over the left side of the chest in order to establish the location of the left border of the heart. Its only real value nowadays is probably in the detection of a pericardial effusion, where a stony dullness is noted.

Percutaneous balloon pulmonary valvoplasty
see *Balloon valvoplasty*

Percutaneous balloon valvotomy
see *Balloon valvoplasty*

Percutaneous transluminal angioplasty (PCTA)
see *Angioplasty*

Percutaneous transluminal coronary angioplasty
see *Angioplasty*

Perfusion defects
see *Nuclear cardiology*

Perfusion pressure
The throughflow in any vascular bed depends on the resistance offered by the bed and the pressure difference between its inlet and outlet. This driving pressure is sometimes known as the perfusion pressure. In cardiological practice the term is most frequently applied to the coronary vascular bed. The level of perfusion pressure in this bed is important because blood flow through the coronary vessels occurs mainly in diastole. When the pressure of perfusion falls below approximately 40 mmHg, the autoregulatory mechanisms which control myocardial blood flow are overwhelmed, the flow declines and myocardial ischaemia ensues.

Pericardial absence
Absence of the fibrous layer of the pericardial sac is a congenital malformation which can occur as part of a more widespread anomaly or in isolation. Absence of most of the pericardium occurs when the heart itself is outside the chest, also as a consequence of congenital malformation (so-called ectopia cordis). An isolated deficiency of the pericardium produces problems more frequently when the defect is small than when it is more extensive. This is because structures such as the left atrial appendage may herniate through small defects and become strangulated. The free edge of small defects has also been implicated as compressing the anterior descending interventricular artery and

precipitating sudden death. Even so-called 'isolated' deficiency is, in one-third of cases, associated with other congenital malformations in the heart and lungs.

Pericardial cysts

These structures, exceedingly rare lesions of congenital origin usually encountered as chance findings at autopsy, are usually classified with diverticula of the pericardium since, in practical terms, the two types of lesion can hardly be distinguished. When large, either lesion may be responsible for palpitations, venous obstruction or compression of the lungs.

Pericardial defects

see *Pericardial absence*

Pericardial disease

A large variety of disease processes can involve the pericardial membranes which surround the heart. By convention, pericardial disease is divided into three main categories: acute pericarditis; pericardial effusion; and chronic constrictive pericarditis. Each one of these categories may occur at some time during the natural history of any disease process which involves the pericardium. See also *Pericardial effusion: Pericarditis*

Pericardial effusion

Any collection of fluid in the pericardial sac is termed a pericardial effusion. The fluid may be a transudate, an exudate, blood or lymph.

Aetiology. The causes of pericardial effusion are legion, but include viral, bacterial and tubercular infections; aortic dissection and acute myocardial infarction; collagen vascular disease; hypothyroidism; malignant disease; post-cardiotomy or post-myocardial infarction syndrome; and an idiopathic cause.

Clinical features. If the pericardial effusion is large, or if it is rapidly increasing in size, then filling of the heart during diastole may be impaired, leading to the clinical picture of tamponade. If it does not impair the haemodynamic function of the heart, then pericardial effusion may be hard to diagnose clinically, the only clue being the fact that the heart sounds may be muffled. The electrocardiogram often shows low voltage complexes with generalized flattening of the T waves. The chest x-ray may show a large globular heart, yet with clear lung fields. Echocardiography is the diagnostic method of choice.

In most cases, echocardiography will show clearly the size and extent of the pericardial effusion and it may also give a clue as to the aetiology, such as demonstrating secondary pericardial deposits in malignant disease.

Treatment. If haemodynamically significant, pericardial effusion may be treated by pericardiocentesis or by the creation of a pericardial window, allowing draining either into the pleural or abdominal cavities. In malignant disease, instillation of cytotoxic drugs into the pericardial sac may prevent recurrences of effusion.

Pericardial friction rub

Pericardial friction rubs are sounds heard characteristically at the left sternal edge where the pericardium comes into close contact with the chest wall. The noises have a superficial scratchy character and may be intensified by pressure from the stethoscope. Usually, the timing is out of step with the heart sounds and, sometimes, may be heard in only one phase of respiration. The position of the patient may also affect the intensity of the sound. Rubs are produced by pericarditis from any cause.

Pericardial knock

This loud and early third heart sound is classically found in constrictive pericarditis.

Pericardial fenestration (window)
see *Pericardiectomy*

Pericardial surgery
Incisions in the pericardium are, self-evidently, an integral part of any procedure which gains access to one of the chambers of the heart during cardiac surgery. When used in isolation, however, the term describes procedures designed to relieve problems originating from the pericardium, such as removal of part of the fibrous pericardium (pericardiectomy) for relief of recurrent effusions.

Pericardial tamponade
see *Pericardial disease*

Pericardiectomy
This term is used to describe the removal surgically of all or part of the pericardium. The operation is performed principally to relieve pericardial constriction. More rarely, it is performed in patients troubled by chronic and recurrent pericardial effusions. A limited pericardiectomy, or pericardial fenestration, is a useful procedure in patients with cardiac tamponade occurring as a consequence of malignant disease.

Pericardiocentesis
This term is applied to the technique of draining percutaneously an excessive accumulation of fluid from the pericardial cavity. The technique utilizes either a sharp needle or a catheter. Classically, pericardiocentesis was performed using a needle introduced under fluoroscopic guidance into the pericardial space from the subxiphoid area, monitoring the procedure both haemodynamically and electrocardiographically. More recently, it has become the practice to use a pigtail catheter introduced by means of the Seldinger technique. This latter method eliminates the prolonged presence of a sharp needle in the pericardial sac

and thus minimizes the risk of cardiac laceration. The main indications for pericardiocentesis include rapid relief of cardiac tamponade and the need to obtain fluid for diagnostic purposes. See also *Seldinger technique in cardiac catheterization*

Pericardiotomy
see *Pericardial surgery*

Pericarditis
Acute pericarditis. The hallmark of acute pericarditis is chest pain produced by the rubbing together of inflamed pericardial membranes. The possible *aetiologies* include viral or bacterial infection; an allergic response to a variety of drugs; irradiation; collagen vascular disease; irritation by blood entering the pericardial sac during cardiothoracic surgery or as a complication of acute myocardial infarction or aortic dissection; and an idiopathic variety. *Clinical features.* The pain of acute pericarditis is often described as severe and knife-like. It occurs in the centre of the chest with an intensity which is affected both by respiration and posture. A friction rub is frequently heard on clinical examination. The electrocardiogram classically shows widespread ST segment elevation with concave upwards morphology of the elevated segments. The treatment is, if possible, the treatment of the underlying disease process. Non-steroidal anti-inflammatory drugs, such as indomethacin, may be helpful in cases of idiopathic or viral acute pericarditis. *Chronic constrictive pericarditis.* In the chronic constrictive variant of pericardial disease, the pericardium becomes a thickened non-compliant shell surrounding the heart. The systolic function of the myocardium is preserved, but the ventricles cannot fill adequately because the heart is effectively occupying a box with fixed volume. Constrictive pericarditis may be a long-term sequel of tuberculous pericarditis, in which

Pericarditis

case the pericardium is often calcified. The constriction may also be found in connective tissue disease, (particularly rheumatoid arthritis); following radiotherapy; or it may occur without any obvious underlying aetiology. The clinical signs of chronic pericardial constriction are a high venous pulse with a dominant X descent, and a loud early third heart sound (the pericardial knock). The only effective relief is surgical pericardiectomy.

Pericarditis, tuberculous
see *Pericardial disease*

Pericardium

The heart is enclosed in a firm fibrous sac, the pericardium, which ensures freedom for its movements and anchors it to the surrounding mediastinal structures. Anatomically, the sac is a double structure. The outer layer, the fibrous pericardium, is thick and is fused to the adventitial layers of the great vessels at their points of entry to and exit from the heart. Inside this layer is the thin serous pericardium, which itself is a double envelope. The outer layer, the parietal component, is fused with the fibrous pericardium. The inner,

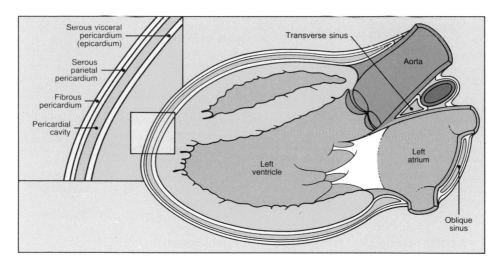

Figure 157. Pericardium. This diagram of the long axis of the heart at right angles to the outlets shows the arrangement of the pericardium. The outer fibrous sac is firmly attached to the great arteries and veins at the base. Within it is a second sac, the serous pericardium. The two layers of this serous membrane are densely adherent to other structures. The inner layer (visceral) is attached to the surface of the myocardium as the epicardium. The outer layer (parietal) is attached to the fibrous pericardium. The pericardial cavity, therefore, is located between the lining of the tough fibrous layer and the surface of the heart.

visceral, layer is fused to the surface of the heart and forms the epicardium. The pericardial cavity is between these two layers of the serous pericardium or, effectively, between the fibrous pericardium and the epicardium (Figure 157). Within the overall cavity of the pericardium there are two recesses, the sinuses. The oblique sinus lies posteriorly and is confined by the orifices of the pulmonary veins and the inferior caval vein. The transverse sinus lines the inner heart curvature between the back of the arterial pedicle and the front of the atria.

Peri-infarction block

This specific conduction abnormality occurs consequent to myocardial infarction. The electrocardiographic changes include a Q wave of 0.04, a QRS complex having a duration in the limb leads of 0.10 and a slurred terminal component to the QRS complex facing the site of infarction. These features of peri-infarction block may be of help in the diagnosis of inferior infarction.

Peroneal muscular atrophy

see *Charcot-Marie-Tooth disease*

Persistent atrioventricular canal malformations

see *Atrioventricular septal defects*

Persistent fetal circulation

This syndrome was first described in 1959 by Richard Rowe (paediatric cardiologist, born New Zealand, practised USA and Canada, 1923-1988). He recognized the features in a full term neonate who became cyanotic 30 minutes after an apparently normal delivery. Chest radiography, electrocardiography and physical findings were normal, but arterial saturation of oxygen was only 66% and angiography revealed massive right-to-left shunting across the arterial duct, with a minimal shunt through the oval foramen. With supportive treatment, the shunt regressed and, by the age of 18 days, all findings were normal. It was over 10 years before further cases were recognized, some proving fatal. Some have now extended the definition of the syndrome to include secondary causes, such as cerebral disease, congenital defects of the lung, hyperviscosity, and so on. In the primary syndrome, however, the cause of the cyanosis is believed to be postnatal persistence of the high levels of pulmonary resistance that exist during fetal life. It is the high pressures within the pulmonary circulation which then promote the right-to-left shunting and produce the cyanosis. It is suggested that the unduly high pressures are due to disorders of blood vessels within the lung, because of maldevelopment or because of altered levels of vasoconstricting agents. Be that as it may, recovery always occurs through a transitional phase, with the shunting becoming bidirectional, then left-to-right and finally ceasing as the duct (and oval foramen) close in their normal fashion. When clinical features of the syndrome are seen, therefore, it is important to differentiate primary from secondary causes. Those with obvious congenital malformations of the lung may not be amenable to treatment. In contrast, most cases of pulmonary parenchymal disease and hyperviscosity are reversible and respond favourably to supportive treatment. Primary disease of the pulmonary arteries may respond to treatment according to its severity. When particularly severe, even the use of potent vasodilators, such as tolazoline hydrochloride or prostacyclin, may be insufficient to prevent progression and death. Most cases, nonetheless, respond to treatment, even if this may need to be prolonged over a period of months.

Persistent left superior caval vein

During early development, the venous channels draining blood back to the growing heart are bilaterally symmetrical structures within the body, the yolk sac and in the placenta. With increasing growth, all of these three systems become lateralized so that single channels drain to the right atrium, the superior caval vein draining blood from the upper body and the inferior caval vein serving as the final common pathway for blood from the lower body, the placenta and the derivatives of the yolk sac. During these processes of growth, the entire left half of the embryonic venous sinus, which initially received the left-sided venous structures, undergoes regression and becomes the coronary sinus. The remnants of the venous structures from the upper body then persist only as the oblique vein of the left atrium and the ligament of Marshall. Sometimes, these structures do not regress and, instead, are found after birth as a persistent left superior caval vein (Figure 158). Almost always, such persistent veins retain their developmental connexion to the right atrium via the coronary sinus. They are then of no functional significance, since the venous return from the left side of the upper body continues to drain to the right atrium. Sometimes, however, the 'party wall' between left atrium and coronary sinus may regress. This leads to venous desaturation, since the left superior caval vein drains to the roof of the left atrium and, almost always, there is an interatrial communication at the orifice of the coronary sinus. Bilateral superior caval veins, each draining to its appropriately sided atrium, are also frequent in the setting of atrial isomerism. See also *Atrial isomerism: Coronary sinus: Vein of Marshall*

arteriosus). They are used to emphasize the subtle differences between the patent duct of an infant who has had full-term development, in which the persistent patency is a congenital malformation, and the patent duct found in a neonate born before full term development in which, with passage of time, and completion of maturation, the duct may be expected to close. Only the first of these contingencies should be described in terms of a persistently patent duct (Figure 159). See also *Patency of arterial duct*

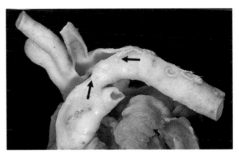

Figure 159. Persistent patency of arterial duct. This anatomical dissection shows persistent patency of the arterial duct (between arrows).

Personality, and coronary arterial disease

It was in the late 1950s that Friedman and Rosenman put forward the concept of a behavioural pattern (which they called type A behaviour) which they believed was related to the occurrence of coronary arterial disease. Since that classical report, many investigators have confirmed to variable degrees the existence of a 'coronary prone behavioural pattern'. The original description of type A behaviour by Friedman and Rosenman was that of "an individual engaged in a relatively chronic and excessive struggle to obtain an unlimited number of things from the environment in the shortest period of time and/or against the opposing

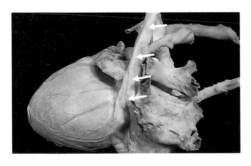

Figure 158. Persistent left superior caval vein. This photograph of the posterior aspect of the heart shows the persistent left superior caval vein (arrowed) running down to the left ventricular groove to terminate in the right atrium.

Persistent patency

These adjectives are almost always, when used in a cardiological context, applied to the arterial duct (ductus

efforts of other persons or things in the same environment". Subsequent studies (for example, that of the Western Collaborative Group) showed that patients with type A pattern of behaviour had approximately twice the risk of developing coronary arterial disease as those without this pattern ('type B' men). Similar risks have subsequently been reported for women with the type A behavioural pattern. It seems that personality acts independently of other risk factors, such as high blood pressure, smoking and levels of cholesterol.

pH, intracellular

The degree of acidity or alkalinity within the cell is an important determinant of myocardial contractility. An intracellular acidosis is associated with an impairment of contractility, while alkalosis promotes increased contractility. The level of these processes, described as intracellular pH, may be determined in a number of ways. The only satisfactory technique for use during life is nuclear magnetic resonance. See also *Magnetic resonance imaging: Nuclear cardiology*

Phaeochromocytoma

Phaeochromocytomas are catecholamine secreting tumours arising from chromaffin cells. Most occur in the adrenal medulla but 10% develop in sympathetic nervous tissue outside the adrenals. Roughly 10% of phaeochromocytomas are malignant. Normally, the tumours occur sporadically. Occasionally, there may be a family history, especially when the tumours are associated with other endocrine adenomas. Their principal cardiovascular manifestation is severe systemic hypertension which may be paroxysmal. The high circulating levels of catecholamines may also produce a myocarditis resulting in left ventricular failure and pulmonary oedema. The diagnosis is made by detecting high concentrations of adrenaline and noradrenaline in the blood or by detecting high concentrations of the metabolites (particularly vanillyl mandelic acid) of these compounds in the urine. If technically possible, surgical removal of the tumour is curative. Prior to surgery, pharmacological blockade with phenoxybenzamine (alpha-adrenoceptor blockade) and propranolol (beta-adrenoceptor blockade) is normally initiated to combat the effects of surges of catecholamines which are released during removal of the tumour.

Phase 4 block

see *Deceleration-dependent aberrancy*

Phenindione

This drug is a synthetic anticoagulant which acts by interfering with the formation of clotting factors. It is effective within 36-48 hours of administration of the initial dose, and its effects wane over a similar period of time after the agent is stopped. Its indications are as for other anticoagulants. Hence, it has been used in deep venous thrombosis, pulmonary embolism, peripheral vascular thromboembolic disease and, sometimes, in patients with myocardial infarction. When it is used in an emergency, the anticoagulant therapy is normally initiated with heparin and phenindione introduced at the same time. When there is less urgency, anticoagulant therapy may be initiated with phenindione alone. It should not be given in the presence of severe hepatic or renal disease, or in patients with potential haemorrhagic conditions. See also *Anticoagulant drugs*

Phenothiazine

The phenothiazines are the group of drugs which are used to treat psychotic patients. They block central dopaminergic receptors and, in many cases, also have alpha-adrenergic-blocking effects. The use of phenothiazines may be associated with a variety of electrocardiographic changes. Arrhythmias, including heart block and ventricular tachycardia, may occur. There are other well-recognized cardiovascular side-effects of administration of phenothiazines, including severe hypotension and the development of a toxic cardiomyopathy.

Phentolamine
This alpha-blocking agent exerts a rapid and potent vasodilator effect, predominantly to the arterial system but also, to a lesser extent, to the venous system. It, therefore, lowers systemic and pulmonary vascular resistances as well as left ventricular filling pressure. It has been used in the past in the treatment of paroxysmal hypertension, and occasionally in conditions associated with acute left ventricular failure. It is rarely prescribed nowadays.

Phenylephrine
This intravenously administered alpha-adrenoceptor agonist has potent vaso-constrictor activity. Infusion of phenylephrine in a dose of 25–200 μgm min^{-1} produces a large rise in arterial pressure and, often, a reflex bradycardia. Phenylephrine is used to maintain arterial pressure in patients with septic shock. Its effects (of increasing both blood pressure and right ventricular preload) make it the choice drug for patients with shock following pulmonary embolus over the period whilst they are awaiting treatment by pulmonary embolectomy or by thrombolysis.

Phenytoin
Phenytoin is mainly used as an anti-convulsant for patients with grand mal epilepsy. It is, however, used on occasions in cardiovascular practice for the prevention of attacks of supraventricular and ventricular tachycardia. It is said to be particularly effective in treatment of arrhythmias induced by digitalis. In practical terms,

the agent is rarely used in contemporary clinical practice.

Philadelphia chromosome
This chromosomal abnormality, in which one of the 22 autosomes has a short arm, is found in patients with chronic myeloid leukaemia. First thought to be due to a deletion, it is now known to be a reciprocal translocation between chromosomes 9 and 22. The translocation produces a transcript for messenger RNA which is an oncogene for the abnormal blood cells.

Phonocardiography
This technique is the graphic registration of heart sounds and murmurs. Such methods were first used towards the end of the nineteenth century as a means of relating mechanical events in the cardiac cycle to sounds within the heart. It was not until the development of the modern piezo-electric crystal microphone, that modern phonocardiography became an established part of contemporary clinical practice. A phonocardiogram is normally recorded simultaneously with the electrocardiogram and with pulse tracings obtained indirectly from the jugular vein or the carotid artery. By this technique, it is possible to establish the timing of the auscultatory and haemodynamic events in the cardiac cycle. Since heart sounds and murmurs vary considerably in their pitch and intensity, recordings are taken at low, medium and high frequencies. Use of a low frequency normally gives the optimal records for normal sounds and for all forms of triple rhythms. The medium frequency is usually used for recording the mid-diastolic murmurs generated by atrioventricular valvar stenosis. High frequency recordings are taken for recordings of second heart sounds, opening snaps, ejection sounds and the early diastolic murmurs produced by aortic and pulmonary valvar incompetence. The main purpose of

phonocardiography is not the detection of murmurs and other events, which is best achieved by clinical acumen, but in the accurate documentation of their positions relative to the cardiac cycle.

Photon-emission tomography
see *Single photon emission computed tomography*

Pick's disease of the heart
(Friedel Pick, Czech physician, 1867-1926)
This eponymous term describes the condition of constrictive pericarditis. There is no good reason for this, because Pick was not the first to describe the condition!

Pickwickian syndrome
Patients with this syndrome chronically hypoventilate, particularly during sleep (sleep apnoea). The resulting chronic hypoxia and hypercapnia ultimately lead to the development of pulmonary hypertension and right heart failure. Characteristically, patients with this condition are grossly obese, oedematous, somnolent and have plethoric faces, in other words they resemble Charles Dickens' description of his fictitious character Mr Pickwick. The first line of treatment is weight reduction, although the use of positive pressure devices nocturnally to assist ventilation may help those patients most severely afflicted.

Pindolol
This cardioselective beta-blocking agent possesses some intrinsic sympathomimetic activity. It is used, as with other beta blockers, in the management of patients with hypertension and angina. Contra-indications and side-effects are as for other agents producing beta blockade. See also *Beta-adrenoceptor antagonists (Beta blockers)*

Pipestem brachial arteries
Calcification of the brachial or other arteries may be a feature of advanced arteriosclerosis. The physical appearance and feel of the vessels thus affected is likened to the stem of an old-fashioned clay pipe. Pipestem brachial arteries may be so severely calcified that they are incompressible by a blood pressure cuff, leading to readings of blood pressure that are grossly and falsely elevated in comparison with the true intra-arterial pressure.

Pirbuterol
Pirbuterol is a beta-adrenoceptor agonist agent with predominantly beta$_1$ activity. The drug is structurally similar to salbutamol and, like salbutamol, can be administered orally, intravenously, or by inhalation. The haemodynamic effects of administration are a mixture of vasodilatation and a positive inotropic action. In the short term, this may be beneficial in patients with heart failure but tolerance to the drug soon develops, possibly due to the down-regulation of beta receptors. Long-term studies show no benefit from treatment.

Pistol shot femoral arteries (Traube's sign)
This sign is auscultation of a loud sound (likened to a pistol shot) over the femoral artery in patients in whom there is a rapidly rising pulse of large volume, as occurs classically in severe aortic regurgitation. A femoral venous pistol shot may occasionally be heard in very severe tricuspid regurgitation.

Pixel
see *Nuclear cardiology*

Planar xanthoma
see *Xanthoma*

Plaque, atherosclerotic
The basic lesion underscoring the appearance of atherosclerotic disease

Plaque, atherosclerotic

is the so-called plaque. The primary lesion on which the plaque develops is initiated by injury to endothelial cells which, under normal circumstances, form a complex barrier. The factors promoting injury are manifold, including effects of shearing and increased concentrations within the plasma of low-density lipoproteins, metabolites, toxins and hormones. This potential for injury is potentiated by other factors, such as hypertension, diabetes mellitus and smoking. Once the endothelial cells are injured in these circumstances, they are unable to cope with the unfriendly environment and provide the nidus for aggregation of platelets and seepage of constituents within the plasma. The response of the tissues to this invasion produces the atherosclerotic plaque, in which there is further proliferation of smooth muscle cells and fibroblasts. Coronary arteries, because of their small lumens, are particularly susceptible to narrowing by these plaques. The fully formed plaque often contains fatty debris, with collagen forming a fibrous cap and separating the fatty constituents from the lumen of the artery (Figure 160).

Plaque fissuring

The histological basis of coronary atherosclerosis is the atherosclerotic plaque. However, formation of the plaque merely narrows the arterial lumen, although this narrowing can produce major consequences in terms of chronic ischaemic heart disease. A much more sinister event is the occurrence of thrombosis within the diseased coronary arteries. Although initially deemed controversial, it is now well established that the event which frequently underscores this process is fissuring, or cracking, of the plaque (Figure 161). The thrombus in such cases is usually found at histology to be attached to a cracked plaque.

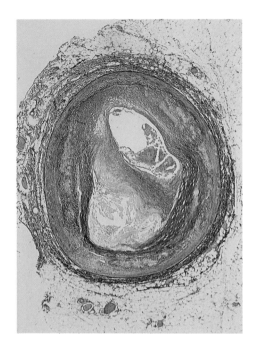

Figure 160. Atherosclerotic plaque. This section of atherosclerosis disease within a coronary artery shows the structure of the typical plaque narrowing markedly the lumen. *(Reproduced with the kind permission of Professor A.E.Becker)*

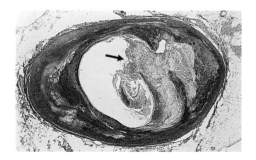

Figure 161. Plaque fissuring. This section of a coronary artery shows a cracked atherosclerotic plaque (arrowed). *(Reproduced with the kind permission of Professor A.E.Becker)*

Plasminogen

Plasminogen is a pro-enzyme that functions as part of the natural process of fibrinolysis. It can be converted to the active enzyme plasmin by the action of several different types of activators. The plasmin thus produced digests fibrin into soluble products of degradation. See also *Thrombolysis*

Plate, cardiogenic

During the very early phases of development, the embryo has the form of a disc, with ectodermal, mesodermal and endodermal layers. Already, at this early stage, part of the mesodermal layer can be identified as the precursor of the heart. This area is called the cardiogenic plate.

Plateau pulse

This wave form describes the carotid pulse and is characteristic of significant aortic stenosis. An apparently normal initial rise is followed by a sustained period, during which the pulse seems to rise very little. See also *Pulse*

Platelet(s)

Platelets are disc-shaped cells which measure 2-3 μm in diameter. There is marked variation in the number of platelets normally present, the range in health being approximately $150 - 400 \times 10^9$ l^{-1}. Their function in the circulation is to reduce leakage of red cells from vessels; to form haemostatic plugs to seal ruptured arterioles and capillaries; and to interact with coagulant proteins to promote coagulation.

Platelet aggregation

Platelets adhere to each other (aggregate) following exposure to certain agonists. Physiologically, aggregation follows adhesion and requires activation of platelets by exposure to damaged surfaces of vessels. Aggregation is essential for the formation of the haemostatic plug, which seals ruptured

arterioles and capillaries. Platelets aggregate in response to agents such as thrombin, adenosine diphosphate, serotonin and platelet activating factor (which is produced by white blood cells and platelets). These agents are all involved in physiological haemostasis. Bacterial lipids, immune complexes, some fatty acids and viruses may also promote aggregation. These latter agents are more likely to initiate activation in pathological processes.

Platelet inhibitors

see *Antiplatelet agents*

Pleural effusion

This term describes the accumulation of fluid within the pleural space. Pleural effusions are broadly divisible into two types, namely transudates and exudates. The fluid of a transudate appears and increases in the pleural space by transudation from capillaries, this being a consequence of osmotic changes associated with either hypoproteinaemia or an increase in hydrostatic pressure such as may occur, for example, in heart failure. The fluid produced has a content of protein of less than 3 g/100 ml. Exudates, in contrast, come from subepithelial capillaries, particularly when these are involved in an inflammatory or neoplastic process. The proteinaceous content of these effusions is greater than 3 g/100 ml.

Plexiform lesions

These lesions, when found in the lungs of patients with hypertensive pulmonary vascular disease, indicate a grave prognosis. They consist of dilated segments of the pulmonary arteries, usually just beyond a branch point, in which the cavity is packed by proliferating cells grouped around slit-like luminal spaces. They develop as a result of fibrinoid necrosis. They are the endpoint of plexogenic pulmonary arteriopathy.

Plexiform lesions

See also *Arteriopathy, plexogenic pulmonary*

Plexus, cardiac
The nerves supplying the heart are derived from the vagus nerves and from the ganglia of the sympathetic chains. As the multiple nerve trunks from the various sources approach the heart and reach its surfaces, they coalesce in the cardiac plexuses, which can be divided into superficial and deep components.
See also *Innervation of the heart*

Pneumonectomy
Pneumonectomy is the surgical removal of a lung. Normally, the procedure is performed to eradicate a cancerous growth but it may also be performed to extirpate chronic infection as in patients with bronchiectasis. The development of atrial fibrillation is a common postoperative complication in patients having had a pneumonectomy.

Pneumopericardium
This relatively rare condition describes the accumulation of air in the pericardial space. It occurs most commonly in association with cardiac surgery, but may also occur in association with traumatic conditions. Examples are ulceration of the oesophagus with fistulous communication to the pericardium; puncture of the pericardium without cardiac laceration during aspiration of bone marrow from the sternum; and in association with artificial ventilation in newborns.

Pneumothorax
A pneumothorax is present when air collects in the pleural space causing partial or complete collapse of the underlying lung. If the air is under pressure, then life-threatening displacement of the mediastinal contents occurs, giving a so-called tension pneumothorax. Pneumothoraces present clinically with dyspnoea and cyanosis, together with the presence of percussive resonance and reduced breath sounds over the affected lung. The chest x-ray normally shows a region of radiolucency on the affected side together with collapse of lung tissue and, if the pneumothorax is under tension, displacement of the heart. In cardiological practice, pneumothoraces are most frequently encountered as a complication of central venous cannulation, including pacemaker insertion, or secondary to inadvertent opening of the pleural cavity during cardiac surgery.

Pockets, endocardial
Thickening of the endocardium is a common pathological finding. One particular type of thickening is the endocardial plaque seen as the consequence of reaction to turbulent flow. When the turbulent flow is itself the consequence of valvar regurgitation, the response of the endocardium is often to form a semilunar pocket. These pockets are described eponymously for Zahn.

Poiseuille's equation
(Jean-Léonard-Marie Poiseuille, French physiologist, 1799-1869)
This equation states mathematically the relation between flow in a long narrow tube, the viscosity of the fluid flowing and the radius of the tube. It is written as

$$Q = \frac{(P_1 - P_2)\pi r^4}{8uL}$$

where Q = flow
P₁ - P₂ = the pressure difference between the two ends of the tube
u = viscosity
r = the radius of the tube
L = the length of the tube

where Q = flow, $P_1 - P_2$ = the pressure difference between the two ends of the tube, u = viscosity, r = the radius of the tube, L = the length of the tube

Examination of the equation shows that flow varies with the fourth power of the radius of the vessel, explaining why, in the body, flow of blood can be regulated so effectively by only small changes in the calibre of vessels.

Polyarteritis nodosa
Polyarteritis nodosa is a systemic disease of unknown aetiology characterized by necrotizing inflammation of the walls of medium sized arteries. The disease may affect only limited segments of the vessels, and has a predilection for their points of bifurcation. Aneurysm formation is common. The cardiovascular system may be affected in a number of ways. Lesions in the coronary arteries themselves may result in myocardial infarction. Alternatively, severe hypertension resulting from renal involvement may lead to left ventricular failure. Pericarditis may also occur. Rarely, haemorrhage into the pericardial cavity may cause tamponade. It is notable that, when polyarteritis nodosa occurs during infancy, the pathological findings are indistinguishable from those found in Kawasaki's disease. See also *Kawasaki's disease*

Polychondritis
The importance of this variant of arteritis is its association with aortic regurgitation due to dilatation of the root of the aorta. See also *Aortic regurgitation*

Polycythaemia
In polycythaemia, there is an absolute increase in the number of red blood cells. This may be a primary abnormality due to a myeloproliferative disease *(polycythaemia rubra vera)* or may be a secondary event due to increased production of erythropoietin. Secondary polycythaemia is commonly found in subjects with cyanotic congenital heart disease where its severity reflects the degree of arterial desaturation. Although an increase in the haematocrit may improve oxygen delivery to the tissues, too great an increase may be associated with hyperviscosity of plasma and elevation of the peripheral vascular resistance. This leads to reduced blood flow within the organs, reduced oxygen delivery to the tissues, thrombotic events and the symptoms of headache, dizziness and roaring in the ears due to diminished cerebral blood flow. Phlebotomy is used to control the haematocrit and symptoms produced in subjects with cyanotic heart disease. The optimal level of haematocrit at which to aim is poorly defined.

Polymyositis
This diffuse inflammatory disease of unknown cause affects primarily voluntary muscles. It also involves various connective tissues, especially the skin and joints. When the disease involves the skin, the condition is called dermatomyositis. The condition is grouped together with the diseases of connective tissue or rheumatic origin because of its overlapping clinical and laboratory features. Involvement of the heart in polymyositis has just begun to be fully appreciated. Cardiac lesions involve predominantly the conduction system, but can also produce an extensive cardiomyopathy and pericarditis. Treatment is by the use of cortiocosteroids and immunosuppressive drugs.

Polysplenia
It is now well recognized that the presence of multiple spleens is part of a syndrome in which the embryo develops two left sides, rather than forming normally with asymmetry between the right and left halves of the body. When describing multiple spleens in this context, it is important to exclude formation of accessory splenic tissue. Accessory splenules are present in up to one-third of all individuals. True multiple spleens (Figure 162) are much rarer. The significance of polysplenia is that the syndrome of bilateral left-sidedness usually involves the heart. In involved

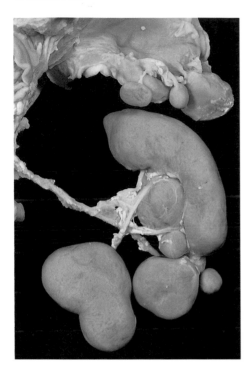

Figure 162. Polysplenia. Multiple spleens, as seen here, are usually part and parcel of the syndrome of left isomerism.

cases, each atrium has an appendage of left morphology and there are other malformations within the heart. Bilateral left-sidedness, however, does not always involve the heart. There is, for example, another syndrome including biliary atresia in which the heart is normal. For this reason, it is more sensible to describe the cardiac involvement in these syndromes, when present, in terms of isomerism of the left atrial appendages. See also *Atrial isomerism*

Pompe's disease
(J.C. Pompe, Dutch physician, twentieth century)
Pompe's disease is a generalized glycogen storage disease (so-called Type II) in which the glycogen accumulates in the heart, the skeletal muscles and the liver. It is due to deficiency of the lysosomal enzyme alpha 1-4 glycosidase and is a progressive disorder. The glycogen which accumulates within the heart affects particularly the conduction tissues. Afflicted children are normal at birth, but muscle weakness and signs of cardiac failure are evident within the first year of life, most babies dying during infancy. Diagnosis is made by confirming absence of the causative enzyme in fibroblasts grown from a biopsy of the skin. No specific treatment is, as yet, available. The disease is inherited in autosomal recessive fashion, so genetic counselling is important. Prenatal diagnosis is also possible by culture of amniocytes. An adult type of the disease also exists in which the heart is spared during the accumulation of glycogen.

Positive end expiratory pressure
Positive end expiratory pressure is a ventilatory technique utilized in many patients following coronary arterial or valvar heart surgery. It is used because of studies which suggest that a positive pressure at the conclusion of respiration produces larger lung volumes and fewer perfused but non-ventilated alveoli. In addition, when used, smaller alveolar arterial oxygen differences are recorded after extubation. The technique is not used in patients with chronic obstructive lung disease for fear of trapping of air and rupture of bullae with consequent pneumothorax.

Positron emission tomography
This technique involves tomographic imaging of positron emitting radioisotopes such as carbon-11, nitrogen-13, oxygen-15, fluorine-18, or rubidium-82. As these isotopes decay, a positron (a positively charged electron) is emitted which is annihilated on collision with an electron with the further emission of two gamma photons in opposite directions. Coincident

detection of these two photons allows reconstruction of the tomograms with much better resolution and count density than is possible from those constructed from the emission of single photons. The value of the technique lies in the radiopharmaceuticals that can be used including ^{11}CO, $^{13}NH_3$, and ^{18}F-deoxyglucose, since these permit flow of blood and metabolism of glucose to be studied quantitatively. Unfortunately, most of these radioisotopes have extremely short half-lives and require an on-site cyclotron for their manufacture. Because of the expense, the technique is limited to only a few research centres (See Figure 139).

Post-cardiotomy syndrome
see *Post-pericardiotomy syndrome*

Post-Eustachian sinus of Keith
(Sir Arthur Keith, Scots anatomist, 1866-1955)
One of the features of the morphologically right atrium is the broad junction of the appendage with the smooth walled venous component. This junction is marked internally by an extensive band of muscle, the terminal crest, from which originate the pectinate muscles at right angles. As the crest approaches the atrioventricular junction, it encloses a recess behind the coronary sinus which is also lined with pectinate muscles. This recess (Figure 163) is the post-Eustachian sinus of Keith. It has no functional significance.

Post-extrasystolic potentiation
Any heart beat which follows a premature ectopic beat is more powerful than the beats which preceded the ectopic beat. This phenomenon of accentuation is known as post-extrasystolic potentiation (Figure 164). Its cause is unknown, but it is independent of the length of the pause following the ectopic beat. A long pause, nonetheless, by increasing filling, can of

itself increase the power of myocardial contraction because of the Starling effect. See also *Frank-Starling mechanism*

Figure 163. Post-Eustachian sinus of Keith.
This view of the right atrium shows the sinus between Eustachian valve and atrioventricular junction (arrowed) which is named for Keith. (OF – oval fossa; SCV – superior caval vein; TV – tricuspid valve)

Post-myocardial infarction syndrome
This syndrome is the occurrence of pericarditis following shortly after myocardial infarction. The attacks occur usually within the first few weeks following infarction, but may occur many months later. The condition is almost certainly due to sensitization to necrotic heart muscle and the prognosis is excellent. There is no specific therapy, and management is normally by anti-inflammatory agents. In rare cases,

Post-myocardial infarction syndrome

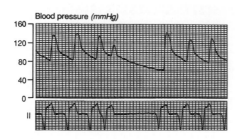

Figure 164. Post-extrasystolic potentiation. Tracings of the electrocardiogram and blood pressure show the augmentation in blood pressure that occurs with the beat that terminated the compensatory pause following an extrasystole.

steroids have to be administered. See also *Dressler's syndrome*

Post-pericardiotomy syndrome

This condition, related probably to the postmyocardial infarction syndrome, may develop weeks or months after surgery on the heart which has involved incisions into the pericardial cavity. It is characterized by fever and pericarditis and can be accompanied by pneumonia and pleurisy. It is thought to be an autoimmune condition and may be recurrent. Anti-inflammatory drugs, such as aspirin and indomethacin, or corticosteroids, may evoke a good response.

Post-stenotic dilatation

This feature is the widening of an arterial vessel immediately downstream to a region of narrowing. Post-stenotic dilatation is classically seen in the pulmonary trunk in patients with pulmonary stenosis. It is also seen in the ascending aorta in patients with aortic stenosis and in the descending thoracic aorta in patients with coarctation. It is thought to be due to turbulence produced by the stenosis which tends to distort the arterial endothelial lining

downstream, thus initiating changes in the subadjacent layers which disrupt the elastic structure of the artery and allow it to widen.

Post-tussive syndrome

A paroxysm of coughing may be accompanied by giddiness, vertigo or syncope, particularly in short, well-built, middle-aged men with chronic lung disease. This is referred to as post-tussive syncope. Syncope in this setting may result, not only from mechanisms mediated by reflexes, but also from hydraulic factors, especially increased intracranial pressure. This latter factor is most important when the coughing occurs in paroxysms. During the paroxysm, pressure within the cerebral vessels declines, first, because of a diminished cardiac output, resulting from reduced venous return due to elevated intrathoracic pressure, and, second, because of the increased intracranial pressure (reflecting the rise in cerebrospinal fluid pressure). Cerebral perfusion declines precipitously in these circumstances and syncope results.

Potassium cardioplegia

see *Cardioplegia*

Potts anastomosis

(Willis John Potts, U.S. paediatric surgeon, 1895-1968)
This anastomosis, used during the early era of surgical palliation of cyanotic congenital malformations such as tetralogy of Fallot to increase pulmonary blood flow, was constructed by connecting the left pulmonary artery to the descending aorta. It is rarely used in current practice, since it is very easy to create too big a shunt, and distortion is often produced in the pulmonary arteries.

Power

Power is a physical term referring to the rate at which work is done.

Practolol

This cardioselective beta-blocking agent is rarely used today because of its serious adverse effects, namely, the practolol oculomucocutaneous syndrome. The agent has been used intravenously for control of arrhythmia in emergencies.

See also *Beta-adrenoceptor antagonists (Beta blockers)*

Prazosin

This vasodilator drug acts by blocking the post-synaptic alpha$_1$ adrenoceptors in vascular smooth muscle. Prazosin can be used to treat systemic hypertension and chronic congestive heart failure, but the development of tolerance to its effects are well recognized. Thus, the drug now finds little favour with cardiologists.

Precordial impulse

This refers to pulsations of the heart beat which are felt on the anterior chest wall. It is usual to palpate both the apex of the heart, which is normally occupied by the left ventricle, and the left sternal border, which corresponds usually to the right ventricular area.

Precordial movement

see *Palpation*

Precordium

This term describes the area of the chest wall enclosing the heart.

Pre-ejection period

see *Systolic time intervals*

Pre-excitation

Excitation of the myocardium in advance of the activation produced by conduction over the normal pathway is known as pre-excitation. It occurs as a consequence of conduction over an anomalous or accessory pathway. In ventricular pre-excitation, the ventricular myocardium is excited prematurely as a consequence of anterograde conduction via an anomalous pathway which bypasses either the entire atrioventricular conduction system (accessory atrioventricular pathway), the atrioventricular node (atrial-His accessory pathway) or the lower portion of the normal atrioventricular conduction system (nodo-fascicular or nodo-ventricular accessory pathways).

Pre-excitation syndromes

These syndromes encompass the combination of electrocardiographic abnormalities which result as a consequence of pre-excitation, producing the tendency for paroxysmal tachycardia. Two forms are best recognized, the so-called Wolff-Parkinson-White and Lown-Ganong-Levine syndromes. See also *Lown-Ganong-Levine syndrome: Wolff-Parkinson-White syndrome*

Pre-infarction angina

see *Unstable angina*

Preload

This term is widely used in both muscle mechanics and in clinical cardiology. It is defined as the force to which the myocardial muscle fibres are subjected in their relaxed state. In the heart overall, the preload can be considered as the pressure within the ventricular chambers at the end of diastole before contraction or, conversely, as the length to which the relaxed muscle fibres are stretched before contraction begins (that is, the end diastolic dimensions or the end diastolic volume of the ventricles). An increase in preload (increased stretch of the myocardial muscle fibres) leads, by dint of Starling's law of the heart, to an increase in myocardial contractility.

Premature beat

This is simply a beat occuring earlier than expected. This implies that the premature beat is ectopic, and may arise from atrial, atrioventricular junctional or ventricular tissue.

271

Premature excitation

Premature excitation of the myocardium occurs as a consequence of an abnormally early excitation (such as seen in the pre-excitation syndromes) or artificially as a consequence of the application of an electrical stimulus to the myocardium. See also *Pacemakers: Pre-excitation syndromes*

Premature ventricular complex

This early depolarization of the ventricular myocardium results from abnormal formation of the cardiac impulse.

Premature ventricular contraction

This term is a synonym for a premature ventricular complex. It is also known as a ventricular extrasystole or a ventricular premature beat.

Prenalterol

Prenalterol was introduced in the early 1980s as a new positive inotropic agent. Pharmacologically, it is a $beta_1$ agonist which is active both in parenteral and oral forms. Unfortunately, its positive inotropic action is weak and, at the present time, it has not found a definite role in the therapeutic armamentarium against heart failure.

Prenatal diagnosis

In terms of cardiological practice, prenatal diagnosis mostly involves the use of ultrasound to detect congenital malformations of the heart. Usually performed between the twelfth and twentieth weeks of pregnancy, in expert hands the technique has proved remarkably accurate, with almost as much precision achieved as in postnatal echocardiography. Initially used for pregnancies at high risk, such as those with ascites or with previous history of congenital malformation, there is now a move towards screening of populations by means of the four chamber section, which reveals most examples of severe malformation. Suspicious cases can then be referred for second opinions in centres specializing in fetal echocardiography. Prenatal diagnosis can also be achieved in some lesions by means of amniocentesis.

Pressor drugs

This jargon term is used to describe any drug which increases the systemic arterial pressure. Most agents thus described are potent $alpha_1$-adrenoceptor agonists (for example, phenylephrine or noradrenaline) which increase blood pressure as the result of intense vasoconstriction.

Pressure

Pressure is defined as the force or stress which is applied to a unit area of a surface. The pressure acts equally in all directions and is independent of the orientation of the surface being considered. Using the International System of Units, pressure is measured in terms of Newton/metre^2 N/m^2, a unit called the pascal (Pa). In conventional cardiac haemodynamics, pressure is measured in millimeters of mercury (mmHg) where 1 mmHg = 133.32 Pa and 1 kPa = 7.5006 mmHg. See also *Intracardiac pressure waves*

Pressure overload

This is a very general term applied to any haemodynamic situation in which a ventricular chamber has to generate a pressure greater than that which is physiologically normal so as to overcome the load facing it. Thus, aortic stenosis is an example of left ventricular pressure overload, while pulmonary hypertension is an example of pressure overload for the right ventricle.

Pressure-volume curves

see *Pressure-volume relations*

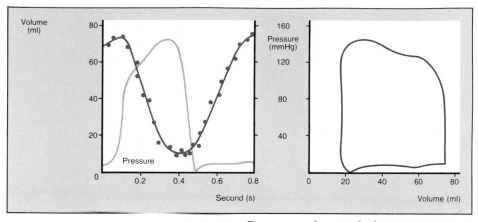

Figure 165. Pressure-volume loop. Volume and pressure changes obtained from a patient with a normal left ventricle are displayed on the left, timed with respect to onset of the QRS complex in the electrocardiogram. On the right, pressure and volume are related to construct a pressure-volume loop.

Pressure-volume loop

If instantaneous ventricular pressure and volume are measured throughout the cardiac cycle, and plotted against each other, then a loop is drawn termed a pressure volume loop (Figure 165). In normal subjects the loop has a roughly rectangular appearance. The uprights represent ventricular pressure change with little or no change in volume (the periods of isovolumic contraction and relaxation) and the horizontals represent the periods of ventricular ejection and filling when only small changes in pressure occur. The integrated area of the pressure-volume loop is the stroke work performed by the ventricle. The area of the loop when expressed as a percentage of the area of a rectangle which just encloses it gives information about the efficiency of the ventricle (normally about 70-80%) in transferring energy from the walls of the ventricle to the blood. See also *Cardiac cycle*

Pressure-volume relations

The manner in which intraventricular pressure and volume changes during diastole is termed the ventricular diastolic pressure-volume relation. Normally, pressure and volume increase together in a curvilinear fashion (pressure-volume curves). The slope of this relation (dP/dV) at any point in time during diastole is the operative stiffness of the ventricular chamber. The reciprocal of this slope is the ventricular compliance. As diastole progresses, the slope of the pressure-volume relation increases, indicating that the ventricle becomes stiffer and less compliant at end diastole. Analysis of ventricular diastolic pressure-volume relations has proved useful in the study of ventricular diastolic dysfunction (Figure 166).

Presyncope

This term describes the symptoms which often occur as a prelude to true syncope, but without loss of consciousness. See also *Syncope*

Primary pulmonary hypertension

This name is given to severe unexplained pulmonary hypertension. On pathological examination, the pulmonary arterioles exhibit intimal fibrosis, medial hypertrophy, fibrinoid necrosis, and the so-called plexiform lesions (dilated side

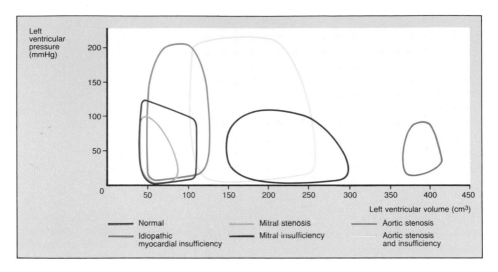

Figure 166. Pressure-volume relations. Left ventricular pressure-volume curves from patients with different types of heart disease. The height of each curve is determined by systolic pressure and the width by stroke volume. The two smallest curves indicate similar stroke volumes; however, in the one for primary cardiomyopathy, the dilated left ventricle is functioning at an inappropriately large volume and the ejection fraction is low. The curve in mitral insufficiency demonstrates volume overload by the large excursion along the volume axis. The shape of the curve in aortic stenosis shows the effect of pressure overload. In aortic stenosis and insufficiency the curve demonstrates the influence of pressure and volume overload, with the large area subtended by the curve.

branches of muscular pulmonary arteries caused by endothelial proliferation). It is these lesions which are recognized by the World Health Organization as the pathological hallmark of the disease. Although its development is unexplained, primary pulmonary hypertension is sometimes found in association with Raynaud's disease, scleroderma, and hepatic cirrhosis. The frequency of its occurrence is increased in those who use the oral contraceptive pill. A virtually identical clinical and pathological picture has been observed in a small proportion of patients taking the slimming drug aminorex fumarate, and it was also seen in victims of the Spanish disaster due to toxic cooking oil.

Primary pulmonary hypertension characteristically affects pubertal or postpartum females. The disease is usually far advanced when it first presents, with symptoms of dyspnoea, right ventricular angina or effort syncope. The clinical signs are those of severe pulmonary hypertension, namely, a loud (often palpable) pulmonary component of the second heart sound, features of right ventricular enlargement and hypertrophy, a raised jugular venous pulse with a dominant 'a' wave, and peripheral oedema. In general, the medical treatment is unsatisfactory, although there are individual reports of reversal of the disease process by anticoagulation, diazoxide, calcium antagonists and continuous long-term intrapulmonary arterial infusion of prostacyclin. In most cases, nonetheless, the disease process is remorseless. Death normally occurs within five years of presentation unless the sufferer is given a heart-lung transplant.

Prinzmetal angina
(Myron Prinzmetal, U.S. physician, born 1908)
In 1959, Prinzmetal described an unusual type of cardiac pain occurring almost exclusively at rest and associated with elevation of the ST segment of the electrocardiogram. This type of angina clearly had a different pathophysiological mechanism from the pattern related to effort, and was shown to be due to spasm of a proximal coronary artery with resultant transmural ischaemia. This syndrome of so-called Prinzmetal angina may be associated with severe cardiac arrhythmias, including ventricular tachycardia and fibrillation, and may result in acute myocardial infarction and/or sudden death. Treatment is by a combination of nitrates and calcium antagonists with avoidance of beta blockers, the latter being the first line therapy in patients with chronic stable angina pectoris.

Following Prinzmetal's initial report, a number of published reports documented the appearance of spontaneously occurring coronary arterial spasm. The concept of vasospasm as a cause of ischaemia was initially controversial, since angina pectoris was thought to be consistently associated with fixed coronary atherosclerotic obstruction in which demand could outstrip supply of the coronary vascular bed. In 1975, however, Maseri published a series of important papers on the clinical, haemodynamic and angiographic characteristics and consequences of coronary arterial spasm. It is now clear that such spasm may be either primary (as in angina of Prinzmetal type) and spontaneously occurring, or may be secondary and superimposed on well defined coronary atherosclerotic

obstructions. A significant body of evidence has now accumulated on the role of coronary arterial spasm as an important factor in a subset of patients with significant organic obstruction. It is, unfortunately, impossible clinically to identify reliably this group. This has led to the development of tests, such as the ergometrine (ergonoven) test to identify the phenomenon. See also *Angina pectoris: Coronary spasm: Ergometrine provocation test: Spasm*

Probe, nuclear
see *Nuclear cardiology*

Probe, scintillation
see *Nuclear cardiology*

Procainamide
Procainamide, which closely resembles quinidine in its electrophysiological effects, is a class I antiarrhythmic drug with local anaesthetic activity. It can be administered by both the oral and intravenous routes, and may be effective in suppressing both ventricular and atrial arrhythmias. Unwanted side-effects include hypotension, gastrointestinal disturbances, hallucinations, a syndrome similar to lupus erythematosus and, rarely, agranulocytosis.

Progeria
This disease of unknown cause produces premature ageing. It is rare for afflicted individuals to survive beyond their second decade. They are apparently normal during infancy, but the disease becomes evident in the second year of life with failure to thrive, loss of superficial fat, scleroderma, alopecia and development of a characteristic facies. There is premature atherosclerosis of the coronary arteries and aorta which results in ischaemic heart disease. Many patients die because of myocardial infarctions, but some have a dilated cardiomyopathy with normal coronary arteries. Calcification of the aortic and

mitral valves is frequent. There is no treatment.

Programmed electrical stimulation
see *Programmed stimulation*

Programmed pacemakers
see *Pacemakers*

Programmed stimulation
The technique of programmmed stimulation consists of delivering critically timed premature stimuli, controlled by a programmable stimulator, to test the electrophysiological behaviour of the heart or myocardial tissues. It is used for both initiation and termination of certain arrhythmias, as well as studying the electrophysiological properties of the cardiac conduction system.

Progressive systemic sclerosis
see *Scleroderma*

Prolapse of valves
The leaflets of either the atrioventricular or arterial valves are said to prolapse when, during their motion, they extend beyond their normal points of closure. In the case of the atrioventricular valves, such prolapse is into the atrium, while arterial valvar leaflets prolapse into the ventricles. The precise definition can be problematic since, because of the overlap of adjacent leaflets, the valves can prolapse to a certain extent without becoming incompetent. Thus, the pathologist may distinguish between hooding of a leaflet and its overshoot, the latter underscoring regurgitation. The discovery by echocardiographers of minimal degrees of prolapse without valvar incompetence must be taken into account when assessing the overall incidence of prolapse. Prolapse is not a diagnosis in itself, since many lesions can underscore its existence, including such lesions as the so-called floppy valve or rupture of the tendinous

cords supporting the leaflets of the atrioventricular valves.

Prolapsing mitral valve syndrome
(*also known as* Barlow's syndrome: Floppy mitral valve syndrome: Systolic click murmur syndrome) The so-called floppy valve (See Figure 83) is a common condition which may affect up to 5% of the normal population. The commonest cause is probably myxomatous change in the connective tissue of the valvar leaflets which makes them excessively pliable and allows them to prolapse into the left atrium during ventricular systole (Figure 167a and b). The clinical manifestations of the syndrome are multiple. The great majority of patients are, almost certainly, asymptomatic. Other patients, however, may present with atypical chest pain or supraventricular tachyarrhythmias. Rarely, patients develop significant mitral regurgitation and, as with any valvar lesions, bacterial endocarditis is a risk. The physical findings are characteristic and comprise a mid-systolic click with or without a late systolic murmur which crescendoes to the second heart sound.

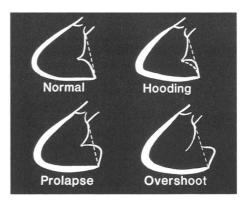

Figure 167a. Prolapsing mitral valve syndrome. This diagram of the leaflets of the mitral valve shows the progress from normality through the features of hooding and prolapse to overshoot of the leaflet.

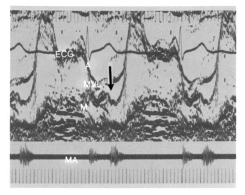

Figure 167b. Prolapsing mitral valve syndrome. Showing classical findings of mitral valve leaflet prolapse. A and M refer to the aortic and mural leaflets. The arrow indicates the point where the mural leaflet prolapses in mid-systole.

These findings may vary with time and with the position of the patient during examination.

Diagnosis is normally established by echocardiography, but care must be taken not to overdiagnose by this means. No treatment is necessary in the great majority of patients, apart from prophylaxis against bacterial endocarditis. Those patients developing chest pain should be strongly reassured. Supraventricular tachycardias are treated in the conventional way. In the majority of those who develop significant mitral regurgitation, however, consideration of surgical intervention is essential. It is likely that a proportion of patients with so-called soldier's heart or effort syndrome (neurocirculatory aesthenia) had prolapse of floppy mitral valves.

Propafenone

This class 1C antiarrhythmic agent is effective for the control of atrial, junctional and ventricular arrhythmias.

Propranolol

Propranolol is a non-cardioselective beta-adrenoceptor antagonist agent. For many years the drug was a first line of treatment for patients with systemic hypertension and angina pectoris. Recently it has been superseded by cardioselective beta blockers, such as atenolol and metoprolol. Administration of propranolol to patients following acute myocardial infarction has been shown to reduce both long-term mortality and the incidence of further cardiac events. Propranolol is also useful in the management of supraventricular arrhythmias, such as paroxysmal atrial tachycardia and paroxysmal atrial fibrillation, particularly when these are induced by exercise. The side-effects of propranolol are the same as for any other beta adrenoceptor antagonist agent. See also *Beta-adrenoceptor antagonists (Beta blockers)*

Prostacyclin

see *Prostaglandins*

Prostaglandins

Prostaglandins are a series of cyclic oxygenated C20 fatty acids whose basic skeleton is that of prostanoic acid. Under present nomenclature they are grouped into four types, A, B, E and F, of which the E and F series are termed primary prostaglandins. The prostaglandins are widely distributed in mammalian tissues, although with considerable qualitative and species variation. Their biosynthesis and release from tissues occurs so readily in response to a variety of stimuli (physiological and pathological) that it would appear that any distortion of the cell membrane is an adequate trigger. They have an effect on virtually every system in the body. The effects on the cardiovascular system are again species-dependent. The E subgroup consistently lowers arterial pressure in a wide range of mammals via a direct effect on peripheral arteries and arterioles. The resulting fall in peripheral resistance tends to produce an increase in cardiac output. Animal studies have suggested that the members of the E subgroup will also increase directly myocardial contractility and, therefore, cardiac output. The cardiovascular effects of the F prostaglandins are more complex, but they are essentially vasopressor in nature. Like members of the E subgroup, they also increase myocardial contractility.

The most commonly used prostaglandin in current practice is *prostacyclin*, preferred mainly for its vasodilatory activity. It has been prescribed in a variety of conditions with varying effect but the most common use is in paediatric practice to maintain patency of the arterial duct. It has also been used in a number of trials in primary pulmonary hypertension where a vasodilatory effect is necessary. Unfortunately, its effects are not consistent.

Prosthesis

A prosthesis is any device or structure introduced to the body to replace a diseased part, or to overcome or bypass a disease entity. Prostheses can be artificial and man-made, or derived from other animal species or from human material.

Prosthetic valve

Diseased valves are amongst the commonest structures replaced by prostheses. Although a distinction is often made between biological and mechanical prostheses in this context, this convention ignores the fact that biological valves are also mechanical. The choice of prosthesis available to the surgeon, therefore, is between a biological substitute or one manufactured from metals, plastics or carbon products. The choice in either group is now vast. Biological prostheses can be obtained from other animal species (heterografts) or from humans, either from cadavers

or as part of a domino chain during transplantation (homografts). Artificial prostheses can be manufactured on the basis of ball valves or tilting discs, with multiple designs in either subgroup. Prosthetic valves are used to replace either atrioventricular or arterial valves, are an integral part of some conduits used in the treatment of congenital malformations, and are an essential part of artificial hearts. See also *Domino operation*

Prosthetic valve endocarditis
see *Endocarditis*

Protamine

This protein is derived from fish sperm and is used to reverse the action of heparin. This antagonistic action is explained by protamine being strongly basic whereas heparin is strongly acidic. Protamine sulphate is normally given by slow intravenous injection in a dose of 10 mg of protamine for each 1000 units of heparin previously administered.

Protodiastole

This is the short time interval occurring at the beginning of ventricular diastole just prior to closure of the arterial valves. It lasts for approximately 0.04 seconds, and represents the time required for reversal of flow in the aorta and pulmonary trunk and for closure of their respective valves.

Pseudoaneurysm

A true aneurysm exists when a swelling of the wall of a hollow structure is produced such that all the layers or the wall are involved. A pseudoaneurysm, in contrast, is produced when only part of the wall is involved in a protrusion or swelling. A good example is when the ventricular myocardium ruptures, but the rupture is contained by the epicardium. Subsequent expansion at the site of rupture, involving only the epicardium, would appropriately be described as

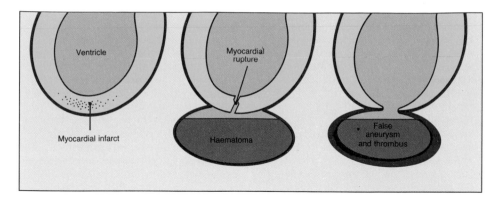

Figure 168. Pseudoaneurysm. The
usual pathogenesis of a ventricular
pseudoaneurysm following: (left) infarction;
(middle) rupture with epicardial limitation;
(right) progression to formation of a false
aneurysm with a narrowed neck.

a pseudoaneurysm (Figure 168). An
alternative name is false aneurysm.

Pseudocoarctation

This term describes the apparent
presence, as seen in an investigation,
of an obstruction within the aortic arch
or descending aorta when, in reality,
the pathway of flow is unimpeded. It is
usually due to kinking of the aorta.

PTCA

Percutaneous transluminal angioplasty.
See *Angioplasty*

Pulmonary angiography

This technique is the injection of radio-
opaque dye into the pulmonary arterial
system in order to demonstrate the
morphology and connexions of the
pulmonary trunk and its main branches.
In the field of adult cardiology the
method is used principally to diagnose
and assess the severity of pulmonary
thromboembolic disease. In paediatric
cardiology the technique is used to
assess the feasibility of surgery in
children with complex congenital heart

disease and to document the presence
and size of pulmonary arteriovenous
fistulas. Dye injected into the pulmonary
arteries passes through the pulmonary
capillary bed and is then gathered by
the pulmonary veins into the left atrium.
This 'laevo' phase of the pulmonary
angiogram can be useful in the diagnosis
of anomalous pulmonary venous
connexions, of left-sided obstructive
lesions such as divided left atrium ('cor
triatriatum') or in the diagnosis of space-
occupying lesions such as left atrial
myxoma.

Pulmonary area

This refers to the area on the chest
where the sounds of opening and closure
of the pulmonary valve are best and most
characteristically heard. It coincides with
the second and third intercostal spaces at
the upper left margin of the sternum.

Pulmonary arterial branch stenosis

Stenoses of the pulmonary arterial
pathways can occur at any point along
their length. They can occur naturally
but, nowadays, are more often the
consequence of surgical procedures
designed to improve the flow of blood
into the lungs. The major areas of
stenosis are within the pulmonary
trunk, at the bifurcation, in the right
or left pulmonary arteries or within the
segmental arteries.

Pulmonary arterial pressure
This is the pressure recorded in the pulmonary arteries. The normal mean pressure is about 12 – 17 mmHg. A mean figure greater than 20 mmHg usually signifies the presence of pulmonary hypertension.

Pulmonary arteries
The pulmonary arteries extend from the ventriculoarterial junction to the capillary beds within the lung. The arterial system thus described can be divided into several parts. The major arterial pathway exiting the heart, and supporting the leaflets of the pulmonary valve, is best described as the pulmonary trunk. It normally emerges from the right ventricle and is anterior and to the left of the aorta, but it can occupy various positions and be variously related in congenitally malformed hearts. Having emerged from the heart, the trunk runs only a short course within the pericardial cavity before bifurcating into the right and left pulmonary arteries. It is these arteries which then extend into the hila of the lung, branching as they do to supply the different segments. The segmental intraparenchymal pulmonary arteries then branch further as they extend towards the alveolar areas. As they pass through the substance of the lung, the individual arteries are distinguished as having pre-acinar and intra-acinar branches, the latter becoming arterioles before feeding the capillary bed surrounding the alveoli. During fetal life, the left pulmonary artery is connected by the prominent arterial duct to the descending aorta but, after birth, the duct becomes converted to the arterial ligament. The major branches of the central pulmonary arteries all have an elastic wall, as do the initial course of the pre-acinar arteries. The arteries become muscular, however, as they approach acinar level, the musculature itself disappearing as each arterial pathway approaches the capillary bed.

Pulmonary arteriovenous malformations
These malformations are abnormal connexions between the arterial and venous systems of the lung which bypass the bed of pulmonary capillaries. The definition can be broadened to include vascular malformations within the lungs fed wholly or partly by systemic arteries which may also connect to systemic veins. The lesions fulfilling these criteria may be single or multiple, and can range in size from microscopic to those filling an entire half of the thorax. Treatment may be conservative, by surgery, or, more recently, by occlusion using techniques of catheterization.

Pulmonary artery-to-systemic anastomosis
see *Shunt*

Pulmonary artery wedge pressure
see *Wedge pressure*

Pulmonary atresia
Pulmonary atresia describes complete occlusion of the channel from the ventricles to the pulmonary arteries. It can occur because the pulmonary valve is imperforate (Figure 169a) or because there is muscular atresia at the outflow tract, the pulmonary trunk then originating above the tri-radiating but blind-ending sinuses of Valsalva (Figure 169b). The consequences of the atresia depend upon the connexions within the remainder of the heart, and pulmonary atresia often accompanies complex malformations such as isomerism of the atrial appendages, double inlet ventricle, tricuspid atresia and complete or corrected transposition. Even when the heart is more-or-less normally connected, however, atresia can still be found in two important settings - when the ventricular septum is intact or when there is a coexisting ventricular septal defect. The latter lesion is almost always the extreme end of the spectrum

of tetralogy of Fallot, and surgical treatment of this variant is constantly improving. Pulmonary atresia with intact ventricular septum, in contrast, still carries a relatively poor prognosis even when treated surgically. Afflicted neonates make up about 2.5% of cases of congenital heart disease. They present with cyanosis in the neonatal period.

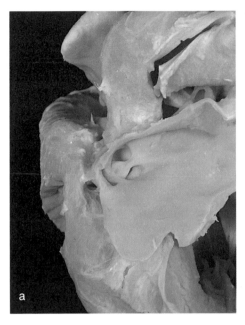

Diagnosis is now made by cross-sectional echocardiography supplemented, if necessary, by angiocardiography. Only those with valvar atresia and 'good' right ventricles are suitable for complete surgical repair. The best that can be offered those with 'poor' ventricles is an initial palliative shunt and a subsequent Fontan procedure. Transplantation may, in future, prove a better option. See also *Fallot's tetralogy: Fontan procedure*

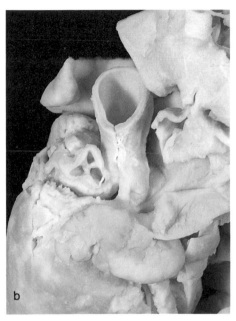

Figure 169. **Pulmonary atresia**. These figures compare an imperforate pulmonary valve (a) with muscular atresia (b) of the pulmonary outflow tract. Note that, in the latter, there is no evidence of the formation of valvar leaflets.

The main problem is hypertrophy of the wall of the right ventricle, which 'squeezes out' the cavity. Generally speaking, prognosis depends upon the size of the remaining ventricular cavity. Those with the smallest cavities also tend to have fistulous communications with the coronary arteries and, in effect, the right ventricle is useless.

Pulmonary atresia with intact ventricular septum
This is one of the two major variants of pulmonary atresia in which the ventricular septum is intact and, usually, the cavity of the right ventricle is hypoplastic. See *Pulmonary atresia*

Pulmonary blood volume
This is the volume of blood present in the pulmonary vascular circuit at any time in the cardiac cycle. It is usually measured by the indicator dilution method, the pulmonary blood

281

Pulmonary blood volume

volume being calculated by means of the equation:

$$PBF = \frac{CO \times MTT}{60}$$

where PBF = pulmonary blood volume in ml
CO = cardiac output in ml min⁻¹
MTT = mean transit time of indicator between pulmonary artery and left atrium in seconds

The calculation of pulmonary blood volume by indicator dilution is beset by a number of methodological problems but most studies suggest that, in normal subjects, the total pulmonary blood volume is in the range of 200 – 300 ml.

Pulmonary ejection click

This is an added high pitched sound which occurs early in the phase of ventricular systole and shortly after the first heart sound. It is best heard in the 'pulmonary area', being characteristically louder on expiration. A click may occur either when there is a minor abnormality of the pulmonary valve, for example, mild pulmonary stenosis, or when the pulmonary trunk is dilated, as occurs in pulmonary hypertension.

Pulmonary ejection sound

This high-pitched noise can be shown by echophonocardiography to occur at the time of initial maximal opening of the leaflets of the pulmonary valve. Such sounds are found when there are pulmonary valvar abnormalities such as congenital pulmonary stenosis, or when the pulmonary valve is normal but the pulmonary trunk is dilated, as in pulmonary hypertension or idiopathic dilatation. Typically, pulmonary ejection sounds occur earlier is systole than do aortic ejection sounds, being found approximately 90 to 110 ms after the onset of the QRS complex. They are also characteristically intensified by expiration and softened by inspiration.

Pulmonary embolectomy

This surgical procedure, involving the removal of clot from the major pulmonary arteries, is usually reserved for life-threatening cases of pulmonary embolism with systemic hypotension and/or cardiogenic shock and arterial desaturation.

Pulmonary embolism

Pulmonary embolism results from the passage of a clot of blood (usually from a peripheral vein) into the pulmonary arterial tree. Rarely, the embolism is due not to clot but to air, fat, amniotic fluid or malignant tissue. The condition is common and has all degrees of severity. The majority of cases are probably clinically silent, but symptoms of pain or sudden breathlessness are indicative. In a number of patients, large amounts of thrombus pass to the lungs and produce a life-threatening situation with systemic hypotension and/or cardiogenic shock. Diagnosis is by ventilation-perfusion scanning and/or cardiac catheterization. Treatment includes anticoagulation for mild to moderate cases and infusion of streptokinase or pulmonary embolectomy for severe cases. See also *Anticoagulant drugs: Pulmonary embolectomy: Streptokinase*

Pulmonary haemosiderosis

see *Haemosiderosis*

Pulmonary hypertension

This situation exists when the pressure within the pulmonary arteries exceeds the upper limit of normal (systolic pressure greater than 30 mmHg; end-diastolic pressure greater than 15 mmHg). Pulmonary hypertension has a number of potential aetiologies. These include, first, an elevation of pulmonary capillary pressure due to increased pulmonary venous pressure, that is, passive pulmonary hypertension. A second cause is a decrease in the cross-sectional area of the total pulmonary vascular bed, due to vasoconstriction (active pulmonary hypertension) or to organic obstructive or obliterative changes. A third mechanism is a marked increase in pulmonary arterial blood flow, often termed hyperkinetic pulmonary hypertension. See also *Primary pulmonary hypertension: Septal defects*

Pulmonary oedema
The accumulation of fluid in the interstitial tissues of the lung and in the alveolar air spaces is known as pulmonary oedema.
Causes. Pulmonary oedema normally results from raised pulmonary capillary pressure, as occurs in subjects with mitral stenosis or impaired left ventricular function, but it may also result from disruption of the integrity of the alveolar capillary membrane. Of these non-cardiac causes of pulmonary oedema, the commonest are the adult respiratory distress syndrome, high altitude pulmonary oedema, neurogenic pulmonary oedema following head injury, toxaemia of pregnancy, or pulmonary oedema following cardiopulmonary bypass (pump lung). Rarely, pulmonary oedema may result from impaired lymphatic drainage of the lungs, as occurs in lymphangitic carcinomatosis.
Symptoms. The cardinal clinical symptom of pulmonary oedema is breathlessness. This is due both to stiffening of the lung parenchyma by fluid in the interstitial space and to flooding of the alveolar air spaces which prevents alveolar capillary gas exchange. It is typical for patients to complain also of orthopnoea, paroxysmal nocturnal dyspnoea, and cough, initially non-productive, but in later stages productive of frothy blood-stained sputum.

The clinical signs that may be observed in a subject with acute pulmonary oedema are cyanosis, an increased rate and effort of respiration, a tachycardia and the presence of fine crackles in the lung bases.
Diagnosis. The clinical diagnosis of pulmonary oedema may be confirmed by the chest x-ray which shows Kerley lines, upper lobe blood diversion and, in more advanced cases, diffuse interstitial shadowing which is often described as having the appearance of a pair of bat's wings.

Pulmonary plethora
Pulmonary plethora is present when pulmonary vascular markings are present over all the lung fields as seen on the chest x-ray. It is distinguishable from pulmonary oedema by the absence of upper lobe blood diversion or Kerley lines. The presence of pulmonary plethora indicates that pulmonary blood flow is increased. It is, therefore, a radiological feature in all forms of significant left-to-right shunting, such as in atrial and ventricular septal defects, patency of the arterial duct, and rupture into the right heart of an aortic sinus of Valsalva aneurysm.

Pulmonary regurgitation
Pulmonary regurgitation is said to occur if blood ejected into the pulmonary artery during systole refluxes back into the right ventricle during diastole. Pulmonary regurgitation may be due to an abnormality of the pulmonary valve, total absence of the leaflets of the pulmonary valve, or to stretching of the valvar orifice by dilatation of the pulmonary trunk in pulmonary hypertension. The murmur of pulmonary regurgitation is best heard in the second left intercostal space or at the left sternal edge. If the pulmonary arterial pressure is high, the murmur has a high-pitched blowing decrescendo quality *(the Graham Steell murmur)*. If the pressure

Pulmonary regurgitation

is not greatly elevated, then the murmur is classically short and low-pitched with a diamond-shaped crescendo-decrescendo configuration. The right ventricle is able to tolerate substantial pulmonary regurgitation over long periods of time, but if the regurgitation is severe, right heart failure ultimately occurs and replacement of the pulmonary valve may become necessary. See also *Absent pulmonary valve syndrome: Graham Steell murmur*

Pulmonary stenosis

Stenosis of the pulmonary pathways can occur within the ventricle supporting the pulmonary trunk *(subpulmonary stenosis)*, at the level of the ventriculo-arterial junction *(valvar pulmonary stenosis)* or within the pulmonary arterial pathways *(supravalvar stenosis)*. Taken overall, pulmonary stenosis accounts for about one-tenth of congenital cardiac malformations, excluding those cases in which the stenosis is part of a more complex lesion such as tetralogy of Fallot. The greater majority of instances of so-called isolated stenosis are due to malformations of the pulmonary valve. Valvar pulmonary stenosis is most frequently due to fusion of the leaflets at the commissures, this process producing a dome at the level of the ventriculo-arterial junction (Figure 170). A significant minority of cases are due to dysplasia of the leaflets. A spectrum of severity can be traced from mild stenosis through critical stenosis to valvar pulmonary atresia. Those with mild stenosis do not usually need treatment and the condition does not progress. The severest forms have a prognosis almost as bad as for pulmonary atresia with intact ventricular septum. It is those with intermediate degrees of severity which need diagnosis and treatment. Most are asymptomatic during childhood irrespective of severity. They are usually discovered because of a murmur, which

is heard maximally during ejection at the left sternal edge in the second intercostal space. A thrill is usually palpable at this site in all but the mildest cases, and the second sound is usually widely split. The chest x-ray, when abnormal, shows prominence of the pulmonary knob and dilatation of the left pulmonary artery but, nowadays, is often normal. The electrocardiogram reflects the severity of stenosis with inversion of the R:S ratio. Diagnosis is confirmed by cross-sectional echocardiography, and the gradient across the valve assessed by Doppler techniques. Catheterization in most centres is now needed only to perform balloon valvoplasty, which is the treatment of choice. Treatment is usually recommended when right ventricular pressure exceeds 80 mmHg, although this level may vary from centre to centre. The results of treatment are excellent and follow-up suggests a normal life expectancy.

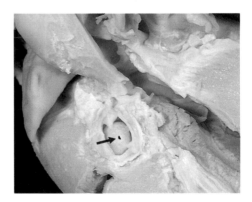

Figure 170. Pulmonary stenosis. In this stenotic valve, the commissures have fused to produce a dome with only a pin hole meatus (arrowed).

Pulmonary systemic flow ratio

This is the ratio of the quantity of blood flowing through the pulmonary circulation divided by the quantity of blood flowing through the systemic circulation. The ratio is used in conditions where there is left-to-right shunting and, hence, exaggerated flow of pulmonary blood. The higher the ratio between pulmonary and systemic flows, the greater is the left-to-right shunt and, therefore, the greater the significance of the cardiac defect.

Pulmonary valvar dysplasia
One of the reasons the pulmonary valve becomes stenotic is that the leaflets themselves are thickened by swollen mucoid tissue. The very bulk of the leaflets then obstructs the ventriculo-arterial orifice. This lesion makes up only a small proportion of all cases with pulmonary valvar stenosis, but is frequent when the stenosis is part of the Noonan syndrome. It is said that this type of stenosis is less amenable to balloon dilatation than typical valvar stenosis. See also *Noonan syndrome*

Pulmonary valve
The pulmonary valve is the arterial valve guarding the orifice of the pulmonary trunk. In the normally constructed heart, its leaflets are supported by the complete muscular infundibulum of the right ventricle. In hearts with discordant ventriculoarterial connexion, however, the pulmonary trunk arises from the morphologically left ventricle. Some of the leaflets of the valve are then, almost always, in fibrous continuity with the leaflets of the mitral valve. These differences in structure of the pulmonary valve, depending on the nature of its supporting ventricle condition, are the substrates of valvar and subvalvar stenosis.

Pulmonary valve stenosis
see *Pulmonary stenosis*

Pulmonary valve syndrome, absent
see *Absent pulmonary valve syndrome*

Pulmonary vascular compliance
This is a measure of the ability of the pulmonary vascular system to distend and increase its volume in response to an increase in intraluminal distending pressure. The compliance of the pulmonary vascular bed in normal subjects is significantly less than the compliance of the systemic vascular bed. In subjects without pulmonary vascular disease, the compliance of the main pulmonary arterial vessels is high, that is, they distend easily as intraluminal pressure rises. In contrast, the main pulmonary vessels have low compliance in the presence of pulmonary vascular disease or pulmonary hypertension of any aetiology.

Pulmonary vascular disease
Changes occurring within the vasculature can be a result of primary disease (primary pulmonary hypertension) but, much more usually, are the consequence of co-existing malformations within the heart. The secondary diseases can affect the arterial or the venous components of the pulmonary circulation. All those lesions affecting the systemic side of the heart, as, for example, mitral stenosis, can eventually lead to a rise in pulmonary venous pressure, and to pulmonary venous hypertension. On the whole, however, the changes on the venous side are not nearly as severe as in secondary arterial disease. Pulmonary arterial changes are the result of increased flow as a consequence of left-to-right shunting across congenital defects, namely atrial or ventricular septal defects, an arterial duct or aortopulmonary window. These are usually divided into pre- or post-tricuspid shunts. The vascular changes occur within the lungs more frequently and at an earlier age with post-tricuspid shunts. There is a spectrum of lesions of increasing severity, often catalogued according to the Heath-Edwards categorization. The severest change is

the so-called plexiform lesion which, when present, indicates that the vascular disease is irreversible. Recognition of the presence of pulmonary vascular disease is of crucial importance when assessing the treatment of congenital malformations with left-to-right shunting, since irreversible disease is a contraindication to surgical correction. See *Heath-Edwards categorization*

Pulmonary vascular resistance
This is a measure of the resistance to blood flow through the pulmonary circulation. It is calculated in exactly the same way as systemic vascular resistance. Its importance is in determining suitability for surgery in patients with congenital heart disease. The higher the pulmonary vascular resistance, the less is the likelihood that conventional surgery will have beneficial effects. When the pulmonary vascular resistance is very high, heart-lung transplantation may be the only approach to certain congenital heart malformations. See also *Systemic vascular resistance*

Pulmonary venous drainage
The pulmonary veins collect the blood passing through the capillary beds of the lungs and return it to the heart, normally to the left atrium, but to other sites when the pulmonary venous connexion is anomalous. The pulmonary veins within the lungs parallel the disposition of the pulmonary arteries, having a segmental arrangement. In the human, their walls are usually thin throughout life. The veins coalesce into four channels which join with the left atrium, two on each side.

Pulmonary venous hypertension
This exists where there is an elevated pressure in the pulmonary venous system. It usually reflects disease on the left side of the heart, either at valvar (mitral stenosis, aortic stenosis) or ventricular level (myocardial disease

of any form). Rarely it is a primary and idiopathic condition affecting the structure of the pulmonary veins. Treatment is aimed at the underlying condition and usually involves the administration of diuretics and/or vasodilators. There is no specific treatment for the primary form.

Pulmonary venous wedge angiography
This little-used technique is used to assess the morphology of the pulmonary arteries in subjects in whom conventional pulmonary arteriography cannot be performed, either for anatomical or technical reasons. A catheter is passed across the intra-atrial septum and wedged in a pulmonary vein. Radio-opaque dye is then injected under pressure which forces the dye retrogradely through the capillary bed and into the pulmonary arteries. The technique is most often used in patients in whom a Fontan operation is being considered, for in these subjects the size of the pulmonary arteries is a factor critical to the success of the operation.

Pulmonary wedge pressure
see *Wedge pressure*

Pulsatile flow
Blood flow in both the systemic and pulmonary vascular systems is pulsatile. This pulsatility of flow is most marked in the great arterial vessels but is still identifiable in the capillary and venous circulations. There is some evidence to suggest that the recreation of pulsatile flow during cardiopulmonary bypass is associated with better organ preservation than is flow at a steady state.

Pulse
When examining the cardiovascular system, it is customary to palpate the brachial, radial and carotid pulses. These may display a variety of abnormalities to palpation which reflect the underlying haemodynamic abnormality. See also

Anacrotic pulse: Bigeminy: Bisferiens
pulse: Collapsing pulse: Corrigan's
pulse: Pistol shot femoral arteries:
Plateau pulse: Water hammer pulse

Pulse deficit
This term is applied to the discrepancy
between the heart rate as determined
from the apex beat and the peripheral
pulse. It is seen in conditions such as
atrial fibrillation where the heart beat is
randomly irregular and weaker pulses are
not transmitted to the periphery. See also
Atrial fibrillation

Pulsed Doppler ultrasound
see Doppler echocardiography

Pulsus alternans (alternating pulse)
This is a characteristic pattern of the
pulse in which the beats occur at
regular intervals, but in which there
is regular attenuation of the height
of the pressures. When severe, the
alternating pulse is so large that the
weaker pulses are not felt at all. The
condition is normally associated with
severe depression of left ventricular
performance and is precipitated by a
ventricular ectopic beat.

Pulsus bisferiens
see Bisferiens pulse

Pulsus bigeminus
see Bigeminy

Pulsus paradoxus (paraxodical pulse)
In normal individuals, the systolic blood
pressure drops by 5-10 mmHg during
inspiration as a result of pooling of blood
in the pulmonary vessels subsequent to
expansion of the lung and the associated
negative intrathoracic pressure. When
the systolic blood pressure falls by
more than 10 mmHg during inspiration,
the pulse is erroneously said to have
a paradoxical character (pulsus
paradoxus). It is, in fact, an exaggeration
rather than a reversal of the normal

situation. The excessive fall of arterial
pressure described occurs classically
in pericardial effusion and constrictive
pericarditis, but may also be associated
with obstruction of the superior caval
vein.

Pump, cardiac balloon
see Balloon counterpulsation

'Pump-lung'
see Adult respiratory distress syndrome

Pump-oxygenator
see Heart-lung machine

Purkinje's fibres (cells)
(Johannes Evangelista von Purkinje,
Bohemian anatomist, 1787-1869)
In hearts from sheep and cattle,
the terminal ramifications of the
atrioventricular conduction system are
made up of cells which, histologically,
are large and appear swollen, having
an apparently empty cytoplasm. These
were the cells first observed by Purkinje.
Subsequent to this description, it has
become conventional to describe all the
cells within the ventricular ramifications
of the conduction system as Purkinje
cells. It is important to note, however,
that these cells in the human are barely
larger than ventricular myocardial cells
and, when properly fixed, do not have the
swollen appearance of the cells seen in
cattle and sheep.

Pyruvate
This compound is an intermediate
substance formed in the cascades of
metabolism. Normal hearts use pyruvate
derived from glycolytic reactions as a
substrate for myocardial production of
energy. The concentration of pyruvate
normally found in the efflux from the
coronary sinus, therefore, is less than
that found in arterial blood. In contrast,
when myocardial metabolism takes place
under anaerobic conditions, the oxidation
of pyruvate is precluded by inhibition

of the Krebs cycle. The concentration of pyruvate within the coronary sinus is then the same as or greater than the arterial concentration.

Q

Q fever

Q fever is an infection caused by the rickettsial organism *Coxiella burnettii*. This is normally a self-limiting condition characterized by fever, malaise and respiratory symptoms. Occasionally, however, it may be a cause of endocarditis. In the latter situation, the disease pursues an indolent course. Blood cultures are negative and the diagnosis is made only by serological testing. Complement fixation tests are used to detect Phase I titres which indicate chronic infection and Phase II titres which indicate acute infection. Should valvar replacement be required, then *C. burnettii* may be cultured from homogenates of the excised leaflets. Q fever endocarditis is difficult to eradicate. The treatment of choice is tetracycline or erythromycin given over a prolonged time interval (one to two years).

Q wave

This term describes the initial negative deflection of the QRS complex. A normal Q wave (for example, Q waves in lead I, aVL and V6) represents activation of the interventricular septum from left to right. Normal Q waves are generally small (<0.3 mV), brief (<30 ms) and no larger than 25% of the R wave amplitude in the same lead. Abnormal Q waves occur as a consequence of myocardial infarction or some other cause of electrically inert myocardial tissue. They will be distributed in the leads facing the area of myocardial damage.

QRS axis

The electrical position of the heart can be expressed as a mean net resultant vector of the QRS deflections in the frontal plane, which is then described as its axis. The normal range is from -30 to +110 degrees for all ages, and from -30 to +90 degrees for those over 40 years.

QRS complex

The surface electrocardiographic manifestation of ventricular depolarization is described as the QRS complex. The normal complex can be described in four vectors. These are, first, the initial septal activation from left to right; second, the overlapping excitation of both ventricles; third, the unopposed activation of the apex and central portion of the left ventricle; and, fourth, activation of the postero-basal portion of the left ventricle and septum. As ventricular activation is largely symmetrical, there is cancellation of forces with the result that only 10–15% of the cardiac potential is recorded on the surface. Normal ranges are well established for amplitude, axis and duration of the QRS complex.

Q-S1 interval

This is the time interval between the onset of the electrocardiographic QRS complex and the phonocardiographic component of the first heart sound produced by closure of the mitral valve. The normal Q-S1 interval measures 30 – 70 ms. This interval may be prolonged in patients with mitral stenosis because more time is required for the left ventricle to build up enough pressure to close the mitral valve against an elevated left atrial pressure.

Q-S2 interval

This is the time interval between the onset of the Q wave of the electrocardiogram and the component of the second heart sound, identified phonocardiographically, contributed by closure of the aortic valve. The time is thus the total time taken up by electromechanical systole. It is one of the routinely measured systolic time intervals. Subtraction from it of the left ventricular ejection time gives the pre-ejection period. The interval is dependent on heart rate and regression equations have been derived to correct for this.

Its duration is shortened by positive inotropic agents and is lengthened by increased afterload or by the presence of left bundle branch block. See also *Systolic time intervals*

Q-T interval

This interval extends from the beginning of the QRS complex to the end of the T wave (Figure 171). It represents the duration of ventricular depolarization and repolarization. In some parts of the heart, however, repolarization may continue after the end of the T wave but, because the area involved is small, is not apparent on the surface leads. The end of the T wave may be difficult to identify precisely. This may be aided by taking the point at which the downslope of the T wave intercepts the baseline. The QT interval shortens with increasing heart rate, and various formulas have been suggested to compensate for this and produce a corrected QT interval (QTc). The most commonly used is the Bazett formula:

$$QT_c = \frac{QT}{\sqrt{RR}}$$

where RR is the interval in seconds.

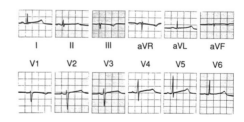

Figure 171. QT syndrome. This simple 12 lead ECG is from a patient with the syndrome of congenital prolongation of the QT interval. The interval is 580 ms.

Q-T syndrome
(*also known as* Q-T prolongation syndrome) The lengthened ventricular repolarization manifesting as a prolonged QT interval sets the scene for life-threatening ventricular tachycardia and for ventricular fibrillation. The syndrome producing such prolongation may be congenital in origin (Jervill-Lange-Nielson and Romano-Ward syndromes) or acquired as a result of various possible mechanisms (bradycardia, electrolyte deficiencies, antiarrhythmic drugs) (Figure 171).

Quincke's sign
(Heinrich Irenaeus Quincke, German physician, 1842-1922)
This sign is a visible pulsation of the capillaries in the nail beds occurring in time with the pulse. When found, it indicates a rapid run-off of a large stroke volume. It is seen most commonly in patients with severe aortic regurgitation, but it may also be observed in subjects with large arteriovenous fistulas or aortopulmonary anastomoses.

Quinidine
This class I antiarrhythmic agent is used mainly in the management of supraventricular tachyarrhythmias, including atrial fibrillation, atrial flutter, paroxysmal supraventricular tachycardia and atrial extrasystoles. It stabilizes the sinus node and, hence, is useful in paroxysmal disorders. It is contraindicated in association with atrioventricular block and in myasthenia gravis.

R

R wave
This component of the tracing of the surface electrocardiogram represents that part of ventricular depolarization that is manifested as a positive deflection.

R-on-T ectopic beats
These beats are recognized on the electrocardiogram as ventricular extrasystoles occuring on the T wave of the preceding beat.

R-on-T phenomenon
This variant of ventricular depolarization is due to a ventricular extrasystole that is timed to depolarize the ventricular myocardium while repolarization from the preceding beat (as reflected by the surface T wave) is still in progress. The ventricle is additionally vulnerable to induction of ventricular arrhythmia during early repolarization and, in certain circumstances (for example, after myocardial infarction), R-on-T ventricular ectopic beats are associated with the induction of ventricular fibrillation.

R-on-T premature ventricular complexes
see *R-on-T ectopic beats*

Radionuclide angiocardiography
The use of a radionuclide (usually technetium-99m) to image the blood vessels and heart. See also *Radionuclide ventriculography*

Radionuclide angiography
The use of a radionuclide (usually technetium-99m) to image the blood vessels. See also *Radionuclide ventriculography*

Radionuclide ventriculography
For this technique, a gamma camera is used to image the intracardiac blood pools following labelling of

the erythrocytes with technetium-99m (Figure 172a and b). Data can be obtained either during the first passage of a bolus of activity through the central circulation (a first pass study), or after the activity is evenly dispersed throughout the blood pool (an equilibrium study). Similar information is obtained from both types of study. The parameters most usually measured are the ejection fraction of the left ventricle and regional motion of the left ventricular wall. Motion of the wall is often assessed from parametric images, such as the amplitude and phase processed in Fourier fashion. Ejection fraction of the right ventricle, volumes and filling rates of the ventricles, and regurgitant fraction in patients with valvar disease, can also be measured. Studies can be performed at rest and during dynamic exercise.

The value of ejection fractions is that they are a simple measure of global systolic function. Since prognosis in cardiac disease is closely related to the amount of functioning myocardium, it is logical to measure these values in all patients, particularly in those where there is a high risk of occult disease, such as those undergoing peripheral vascular surgery. Even if cardiac catheterization and x-ray ventriculography are planned, measurement of ejection fractions by radionuclide ventriculography is wise, since visual assessment may be misleading unless area-length measurements are made on biplane ventriculograms. The x-ray ventriculogram may even be considered unnecessary following a good quality radionuclide ventriculogram. Other patients in which noninvasive measurements of ejection fractions may be valuable are those with left ventricular failure of any aetiology. Clinical assessment of left ventricular function in this setting may be very unreliable and, in those receiving cardiotoxic chemotherapy, larger cumulative doses

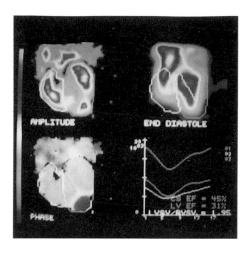

Figure 172a. Radionuclide ventriculography (end diastole). The end diastolic image shows a dilated left ventricle while the curves show a reduced ejection fraction of 45%. The amplitude image shows reduced values (hypokinesia) in the anteroseptal region, and the phase image shows a discrete area of apical dyskinesis indicating an apical aneurysm. *(Reproduced with the kind permission of Dr R.Underwood)*

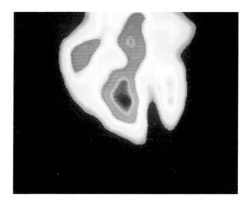

Figure 172b. Radionuclide ventriculography. This left anterior oblique image of the intracardiac blood pools shows normal left (4 o'clock) and right ventricles (7 o'clock). *(Reproduced with the kind permission of Dr R.Underwood)*

may be given if ventricular function is monitored. See also *Nuclear cardiology: Technetium-99m*

Rashkind procedure
(William Rashkind, American paediatric cardiologist, 1922-1986)
Prior to the 1960s, patients with complete transposition (the combination of concordant atrioventricular and discordant ventriculoarterial connexions) had a dreadful prognosis. However, in 1966, Rashkind and Miller described the technique in which a balloon catheter was placed, via venous access, across the atrial septum, inflated in the left atrium and then pulled back into the right atrium, thus rupturing the atrial septum and permitting admixture of pulmonary and systemic venous blood streams. It was this procedure of balloon atrial septostomy which heralded the remarkable advances made over the last 25 years in treatment of patients with complete transposition and related conditions. As Rashkind himself remarked, the success of the procedure is related to the jerk on the end of the catheter!

Rastelli classification
(Gian Carlo Rastelli, Italian cardiac surgeon, domiciled in USA, 1933-c1969)
One of the variable features in hearts with an atrioventricular septal defect is the morphology of the two leaflets of the common atrioventricular valve which bridge the ventricular septum. The particular patterns of tethering of the superior of these leaflets were highlighted in a seminar paper published from the Mayo Clinic in 1966 in which the first author was Rastelli.
He and his colleagues identified three patterns, dubbed A through C, which, in essence, described increasing degrees of containment of the superior bridging leaflet within the right ventricle, together with variability in arrangement of the papillary muscle supporting the right

ventricular end of the leaflet. Initially considered of major surgical significance, the importance of the classification has waned in recent years.

Rastelli procedure
(Gian Carlo Rastelli, Italian cardiac surgeon, 1933-c1969)
At about the same time as he and his colleagues studied and described the atrioventricular valves in atrioventricular septal defects, Rastelli and his associates also pioneered the use of external valved conduits in the repair of congenitally malformed hearts. This technique, first described by them in a patient with complete transposition, ventricular septal defect, and subpulmonary stenosis, consisted of closing the defect so that the aorta was connected to the left ventricle, closing the pulmonary trunk and placing a valved conduit between the right ventricle and the distal pulmonary arteries (Figure 173). A similar technique was subsequently used in patients with common arterial trunk. The techniques are not easy to implement and, even in the best centres, still carry mortality rates of around 10%.

Raynaud's phenomenum
(Maurice Raynaud, French physician, 1834-1881)
Raynaud's phenomenum is characterised by intermittent pallor and/or cyanosis of the extremities precipitated by exposure to cold. In some cases where the condition is particularly severe and chronic the skin overlying the fingers and the nails becomes atrophic. The condition normally represents a hyperactive vasomotor condition but, in rare cases, it may be associated with primary pulmonary hypertension, scleroderma and coronary arterial spasm.

Receptors, alpha and beta
see *Adrenoceptors*

Re-entry

This mechanism of tachycardia, originally conceptualized by Mines in 1914, is based on the fact that, under certain circumstances, an impulse may circulate continously around a closed circuit of myocardium, thus perpetuating itself. The primary pre-requisite for re-entry is the development of unidirectional block in tissues with disparate electrophysiological properties.

recovered its excitability from the previous depolarization.

Refractory period

This is the period following a depolarization when myocardial tissue cannot be stimulated to elicit a normal action potential (Figure 174). Different measurements of refractoriness may be obtained, and refractory periods must be considered differently in

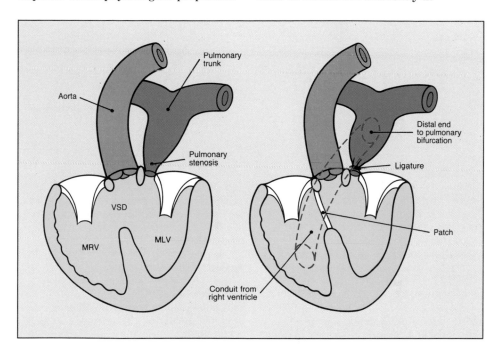

Figure 173. Rastelli procedure. This diagram shows the steps involved in the Rastelli procedure for patients with the combination of complete transposition, ventricular septal defect and subpulmonary stenosis. (MRV – morphological right ventricle; MLV – morphological left ventricle; VSD – ventricular septal defect)

It is also implicit that conduction through the circuit can occur only when it travels sufficiently slowly to allow each subsequent area to have

measurements from single cells and those obtainable from groups of cells. The single cell demonstrates a zone of relative refractoriness in response to premature stimulation in which an action potential can be elicited but which has different characteristics from the action potential obtained later in diastole when the cell has fully recovered. The absolute refractory period defines the longest coupling interval at which a premature stimulus fails to elicit an action potential. In intact myocardial

Refractory period

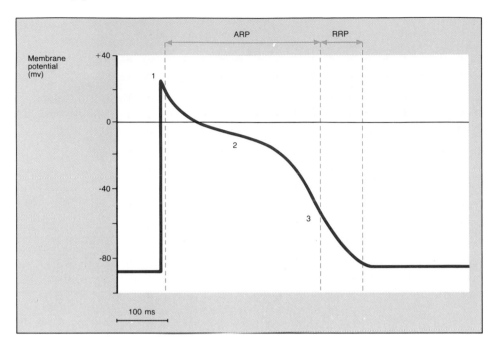

Membrane
potential
(mv)

ARP   RRP

+40
0
-40
-80

1
2
3

100 ms

Figure 174. Refractory period. Once depolarized, the cardiac cells remain absolutely refractory until Phase 3 of the action potential when the cell becomes relatively refractory. At the end of Phase 3 the cell becomes normally responsive. (ARP – absolute refractory period; RRP – relative refractory period)

tissue, it is usual to define effective, functional and relative refractory periods. The effective refractory period is the longest coupling interval of a premature stimulus which does not produce a propagated response. The functional refractory period describes the ability of tissue to conduct a premature response. This is defined as the shortest interval between propagated responses to any premature interval. The relative refractory period describes the ability of myocardial tissue to conduct premature impulses more slowly than during the fully repolarized state. This is defined as the coupling interval of a premature

stimulus at which conduction delay appears relative to the conduction of premature stimulation in the fully repolarized state.

Refsum's disease
(Sigvald Bernhard Refsum, Norwegian physician, born 1907)
This autosomal recessive disorder of lipid metabolism is characterized by an accumulation of phytanic acid within the tissues. Cardiovascular involvement is common, and involves both myocardial cells and conduction tissues. Myocardial cells become atrophic and there is increased intercellular fibrosis. The autonomic nerves to the heart, the sinus node and the atrioventricular bundle become abnormally prominent due to accumulation of the phytanic acid in the myelin sheath. In association with cardiovascular involvement there is also neurological involvement, particularly that of chronic polyneuropathy, cerebellar ataxia and retinitis pigmentosa.

The electrocardiogram may show conduction and repolarization defects of any degree of abnormality, up to and including complete heart block. Treatment is by diet, using one which is low in phytanic acid, together with standard antiarrhythmic therapy as necessary.

Regurgitation
Regurgitation is a pseudonym for a leak through one of the cardiac valves. See also *Aortic regurgitation: Mitral regurgitation: Pulmonary regurgitation: Tricuspid regurgitation*

Reiter's syndrome
(Hans Conrad Julius Reiter, German physician, 1881-1969)
This disease is characterized by the triad of arthritis, conjunctivitis and urethritis. Its exact aetiology is unknown but it is found in association with sexually transmitted chlamydial infections or following diarrhoeal illnesses. A preponderance of patients with Reiter's syndrome have the HLA B27 genotype. A very small proportion of patients develop myocarditis or an aortitis leading to dilatation of the aortic root and aortic regurgitation.

Rejection
As with transplantation of any organ, patients after heart and heart-lung transplantation require permanent immunosuppression. This needs to be most intense during the first few months after transplantation, when acute rejection is most prevalent. Until a few years ago, most centres used conventional immunotherapy, with steroids and azathioprine. Since 1982, however, cyclosporin has formed the basis of most immunosuppressive protocols. It reduces the incidence of episodes of rejection. Those episodes that do occur tend to be less acute and more readily reversed. This results in an improved probability of survival,

fewer serious bacterial infections and a reduced length of stay in hospital, leading to lower costs. There are, nonetheless, a number of complications to the use of cyclosporin. Its side-effects include nephrotoxicity and systemic hypertension. A possible future solution to these problems is the development of a non-nephrotoxic analogue of cyclosporin.

Remak's ganglion
(Robert Remak, German anatomist, 1815-1865)
This is a large conglomeration of nervous tissue found in the amphibian heart. Its significance is historic rather than scientific.

Renin-angiotensin-aldosterone system
The renin-angiotensin-aldosterone system provides a homeostatic mechanism by which the body regulates blood pressure and plasma volume. Renin is a proteolytic enzyme secreted by juxtaglomerular cells in a concentration which is inversely related to the pressure in the efferent arterials supplying them. It cleaves substrate protein in the plasma to form the biologically inactive decapeptide angiotensin I. Angiotensin I is transformed to the biologically active octopeptide angiotensin II by angiotensin converting enzyme present in the lung. Angiotensin II has two main actions. Firstly, it is a potent vasoconstrictor. Secondly, it stimulates cells in the adrenal cortex to secrete the hormone aldosterone. Aldosterone, in turn, acts on the distal convoluted tubules and collecting ducts in the kidney to promote salt and, therefore, water retention.

Reperfusion
It is well established from experimental studies that reperfusion of myocardial cells after a critical period of ischaemia has a markedly deleterious effect. The morphologic manifestation is the clumping of the contractile elements

which produces so-called contraction band necrosis. These changes are of significance in reperfusion occurring in the setting of classical myocardial infarction, but particularly in relation to restoration of blood flow after cardiopulmonary bypass. Although it was initially thought that contraction band necrosis occurred only in cells destined to die, it is now known that the cells can be revitalized by restoration of flow. The restoration, however, must be achieved shortly after the onset of infarction or, alternatively, the metabolic demand be reduced so that reperfusion occurs at an early stage as far as the processes of metabolism are concerned. See also *Contraction bands*

Reserpine

This alkaloid compound is derived from the root of the climbing shrub *Rauwolfia serpentina*, a native of the Indian sub-continent. The drug has a potent hypotensive action. It causes peripheral vasodilatation by depleting the post-ganglionic adrenergic neurones of noradrenaline, and it also acts centrally by depleting stores of catecholamines in the central nervous system. Reserpine is now seldom used in cardiological practice, principally because of its high incidence of side-effects. These include thrombocytopenia and pericarditis. It also carries a risk of precipitating hypertensive crises if given inadvertently and concurrently with inhibitors of monoamine oxidase.

Resistance

Vascular resistance is defined as mean pressure drop across the vascular bed divided by the mean flow through that bed. Resistance is normally expressed in terms of arbitrary units called Wood units or as dynes/s/cm^2.

Respiratory distress syndrome

see *Adult respiratory distress syndrome*

Resting length-tension relation

Progressive stretching of relaxed heart muscles results in a rise in tension which increases exponentially. The slope of this relation (the change in tension versus the change in length) reflects the stiffness of the muscle. Some of the factors which alter the relation are age, ischaemia and tachycardia.

Resting membrane potential

The portion of the transmembrane action potential between the end of repolarization and the onset of depolarization is said to be the resting potential, arbitrarily referred to as Phase 4. In atrial or ventricular myocardial cells, the potential rests at -80 to -90 mV until the cell is stimulated. Cells of the sinus and atrioventricular nodes do not rest at a fixed membrane potential during diastole but demonstrate spontaneous diastolic depolarization, so-called Phase 4 depolarization.

Restrictive cardiomyopathy

Although in the 1980 report of the task forces of the World Health Organization and the International Society of Federations of Cardiology, the term restrictive cardiomyopathy is used interchangeably with obliterative cardiomyopathy, this is less than satisfactory. The obliterative cardiomyopathies are characterized by conditions such as endomyocardial fibrosis and Löffler's fibroplastic endocarditis. In contrast, it is cardiac amyloidosis which exemplifies the restrictive (or constrictive) variant of cardiomyopathy. The myocardium throughout the heart is loaded with deposits of amyloid, thus producing reduced contractility and restricting its function.

Resuscitation, cardiopulmonary

see *Cardiopulmonary resuscitation*

Revascularization

This term describes the restoration of blood flow to any organ. In the heart, it can occur naturally as a consequence of the development of collateral channels, or can be the result of therapeutic intervention, either surgically or by thrombolysis or similar procedures.

Rhabdomyoma

The rhabdomyoma, a benign growth, is the most frequent cardiac tumour found in infants and children, accounting for about half of all tumours found in the heart during the first year of life. They are frequently seen in concert with tuberous sclerosis. The tumour tissue is composed of swollen myocytes in which the nucleus is suspended centrally by bands of contractile material, hence the term 'spider cells' (Figure 175). They probably represent a hamartomatous change of the cells. The symptoms reflect the size of the tumour, and patients can present as stillbirths, with congestive heart failure or with arrhythmias. Some may be amenable to surgical excision but, often, because of its location, complete removal is impossible.

Rhabdomyosarcoma

This tumour is the rare malignant variant of the rhabdomyoma, and is seen in infants and children. Clinically, the tumour has a rapid downhill course with death usually occurring soon after the onset of symptoms. As yet, there is no suitable treatment.

Rheumatic carditis

This term describes the involvement of the heart in the acute and chronic phases of rheumatic heart disease. All layers of the heart can be, and usually are, involved, or else the disease can be described in terms of its effects on the pericardium, myocardium, valves or endocardium. See also *Rheumatic fever (and rheumatic heart disease)*

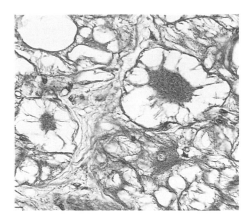

Figure 175. Rhabdomyoma. This photomicrograph shows the spider cells which are the typical feature of the tumour. *(Reproduced with the kind permission of Professor A.E.Becker)*

Rheumatic fever (and rheumatic heart disease)

Rheumatic fever is usually classified as a disease of connective tissues, since its anatomic hallmark is damage to collagen fibrils and to the ground substance of connective tissue (especially in the heart).

Aetiology. The condition follows infection with Group A streptococcus due to development of an anti-streptococcal antibody that cross-reacts with connective tissue.

Clinical features. There has been a dramatic decline in the incidence and prevalence of this condition in the civilized world in the last decade, which is thought to be related to an improvement in social conditions. In contrast, the disease is still endemic in less well-developed countries. It can involve almost any system in the body but particularly affected are the central nervous system (chorea), the cardiovascular system (endocarditis, myocarditis, pericarditis and atrioventricular conduction blocks) and the skin (erythema marginatum).

297

Rheumatic fever

From the cardiological viewpoint, pancarditis is almost always evident at the stage of acute infection, with signs and symptoms of pericarditis, myocarditis and endocarditis all being evident. Despite the high incidence of prolongation of atrioventricular conduction during the acute phase of rheumatic fever, visible changes in the atrioventricular conduction tissues are seen in only the minority of autopsy cases, suggesting that heart block is functional rather than structural in nature. In the long term, the major impact on the heart is the development of valvar deformities, most commonly producing mitral stenosis and/or regurgitation across the aortic and mitral valves. Right-sided lesions, however, are not uncommon. The resulting problems of valvar stenosis and regurgitation are dealt with in detail elsewhere in this dictionary.

Investigations. Although there are no pathognomonic tests for rheumatic fever, laboratory findings are helpful in two ways. The first is to establish the anticedent streptococcal infection (ASOT titres) while the second is to document the presence or persistence of an inflammatory process (for example, white blood cells, erythrocyte sedimentation rate, C-reactive protein). For clinical diagnosis of the acute infection, T.Duckett Jones in 1944 produced a list of both major and minor manifestations. The finding of two major (or one major and two minor) manifestations indicates a high probability of acute infection.

Treatment may be subdivided into general management and antirheumatic therapy. General management involves committing the patient to bed for the duration of the acute febrile portion of the illness and then ensuring rest until clinical and laboratory evidence indicates abatement of inflammation. Use of antirheumatic agents is not critical to the outcome of most attacks of rheumatic fever, but corticosteroids and salicylates can be regarded as valuable symptomatic and supportive therapy. Patients without carditis may be treated with analgesics only. When carditis is present, it is normal to prescribe corticosteroids in addition. Neither corticosteroids nor salicylates shorten the course of rheumatic fever, but the duration of therapy must be estimated according to the expected course of the attack. Approximately 80% of most attacks subside within about six weeks, 90% within twelve weeks and only about 5% will persist for more than six months. After the acute attack has abated, it is normal to use secondary antibacterial prophylaxis, utilizing a single monthly intramuscular injection of 1.2 million units of benzathine penicillin G until either the age of puberty or the early twenties. See also *Jones criteria*

Rib notching
see *Notching of ribs, in coarctation of aorta*

Rickettsial endocarditis
This variant of endocarditis is one which follows infection by a rickettsial organism, such as those responsible for Q fever or Rocky Mountain spotted fever. See also *Q fever*

Right bundle branch
Having penetrated through the central fibrous body, the axis of atrioventricular conduction tissue splits into its right and left branches. The left branch is an extensive fan-like structure. In contrast, the right bundle is a narrow cord of cells which divides from the axis beyond the last point of descent of the left branch. The cord burrows through the septum, emerging on the right surface in relation to the medial papillary muscle (Figure 176). It then continues as a narrow cord down the body of the septomarginal trabeculation before ramifying into the myocardium at the ventricular apex. One of its branches crosses to the anterior

papillary muscle of the tricuspid valve within the moderator band.

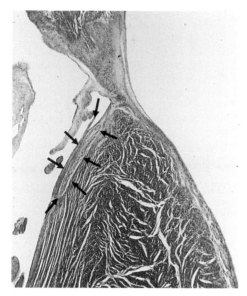

Figure 176. Right bundle branch. The cord-like right bundle branch is seen on the right ventricular aspect of the septal surface (arrowed). *(Reproduced with the kind permission of Professor A.E.Becker)*

Right bundle branch block
This abnormal pattern of atrioventricular conduction reflects interruption of a supraventricular impulse as it traverses the right bundle branch such that depolarization of the right ventricle results from slow transmyocardial spread of activation from the centre and left ventricle. The late and unopposed right ventricular activation produces a characteristic pattern on the surface electrocardiogram, notably an RSR pattern in lead V1. (See Figure 33)

Right-sided aorta
In the normal person, the aorta emerges from the base of the heart to the right of the pulmonary trunk but then crosses the left bronchus and descends through the

thorax on the left side of the vertebral column. Such left-sided aortae are also found in the majority of patients with congenital cardiac malformations. In a minority of cases, however, the aortic arch crosses the right bronchus as it passes into the posterior mediastinum. Even though the descending aorta may subsequently cross to the left, the crossing of the right bronchus is the criterion for diagnosis of a right aortic arch. It is the rule in patients with mirror-image arrangement of the organs, and is frequently seen in those with isomerism of the atrial appendages. In those patients with usual atrial arrangement (solitus), a right aortic arch is found most frequently with tetralogy of Fallot or common arterial trunk. The right-sided location of the ascending aorta is also important in patients with congenitally malformed hearts. Normally, the aorta is right-sided relative to the pulmonary trunk as it emerges from the base of the heart, but is posteriorly located. An anterior and right-sided aorta is the typical finding in patients with complete transposition or double outlet from the right ventricle, but is not specific for these conditions.

Right ventricle
This ventricle is so named because, in the normal person, it is rightward to its partner. It is the ventricle supporting the pulmonary circulation and contains the tricuspid and pulmonary valves. Its most constant feature when malformed, however, is the presence of coarse apical trabeculations (Figure 177).

Right ventricle, double-outlet
see *Double outlet ventricle*

Right ventricular hypertrophy
Hypertrophy of the right ventricle is one of the cardiac responses to either acquired or congenital heart disease. The right ventricle typically becomes hypertrophied with *cor pulmonale* or in

Right ventricular hypertrophy

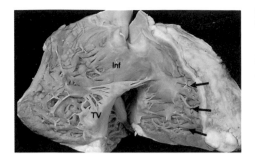

Figure 177. Right ventricle. This picture shows the coarse apical trabeculations (arrowed) which are the typical feature of the morphologically right ventricle. (Inf – infundibulum; TV – tricuspid valve)

the presence of pulmonary hypertension. It can become involved in the process of hypertrophic cardiomyopathy, although this is rare. Right ventricular hypertrophy is a cardinal feature of congenital lesions such as tetralogy of Fallot and pulmonary atresia with intact ventricular septum. The hypertrophy manifests itself with typical electrocardiographic patterns.

Right ventricular infarction

Right ventricular infarction is rare, as an isolated lesion, but it commonly accompanies inferior or true posterior left ventricular infarction. Clinical diagnosis is based upon a constellation of clinical findings, including elevated jugular venous pressures with a dominant V wave and steep Y descent, right ventricular third or fourth heart sounds and a positive Kussmaul's sign. The condition can be diagnosed on the basis of ST segment elevation in lead V4R. Treatment differs from that of left ventricular infarction, since when there is significant right ventricular damage it is often necessary to maintain a high filling pressure and, therefore, infusion of fluids may be necessary to expand the circulation. Another common association is the development of atrioventricular

nodal block. When infarction is extensive, the patient may develop cardiogenic shock.

Right ventricular inflow tract

The inflow tract of the right ventricle surrounds and supports the morphologically tricuspid valve. Its anatomic characteristics are the presence of attachments of tendinous cords to the ventricular septum along with the eccentric arrangement of medial, anterior and inferior papillary muscles.

Right ventricular outflow tract obstruction

The features producing obstruction within the outflow tract of the right ventricle are underscored by the fact that, almost without exception, the leaflets of the arterial valve of the right ventricle are supported by a complete muscular infundibulum. The obstruction, therefore, is most usually muscular, either of tubular and concentric form when the ventricular septum is intact, or due to anterior deviation of the outlet septum when there is a coexisting ventricular septal defect. Such muscular obstruction is amenable to surgical excision but, when extreme, is often accompanied by a hypoplastic ventriculoarterial junction. In these circumstances, it is usually necessary to augment the resection by use of a transjunctional patch or, rarely, an extracardiac conduit. Obstruction of the outflow tract can more rarely be due to aneurysmal dilatation of adjacent fibrous structures, such as accessory leaflets of the tricuspid valve, the membranous septum or even the Eustachian valve of the right atrium. Hypertrophy of apical trabeculations (so-called two-chambered right ventricle) can also obstruct the opening of the outlet component. Some component of valvar obstruction is almost always present in addition to any form of subvalvar obstruction. See also *Spinnaker syndrome*

300

Ring, vascular
see *Vascular ring*

Roger's disease
(Henri Louis Roger, French physician, 1809-1891)
This term was formerly for description of an isolated ventricular septal defect, recognizing the role of Henri Roger in describing its clinical manifestations.

Rolled edge deformity
Syphilitic infection produces a highly characteristic appearance of the leaflets of the aortic valve. The leaflets become fibrotic and retracted with widening of the commissures, the arrangement of the leaflets being appropriately likened to a rolled edge. The deformity is now rarely seen in the Western world because of the infrequency of chronic syphilitic disease.

Romaña's sign
(Cecilio Romaña, Argentinian physician, born 1899)
This finding of unilateral periorbital oedema results from acute infection by *Trypanosoma cruzi*, the causative agent for Chagas' disease. It occurs because the reduviid bug (the vector of the disease) frequently bites humans around the eyes. *Trypanosoma cruzi*, excreted in the bug's faeces, then enter the body, either through abraded skin or the conjunctiva, and cause a local inflammatory response. See also *Chagas' disease*

Romano-Ward syndrome
(20th century physicians)
In the early 1960s, Romano and Ward described independently the association of hereditary prolongation of the Q-T interval of the electrocardiogram and syncope or sudden death. The coupling of these features in children who were also deaf had been noted earlier by Jervell and Lange-Nielsen, but the Romano-Ward syndrome is found in those with normal hearing. It is also inherited in autosomal dominant fashion,

while the syndrome is autosomally recessive in those who are deaf.

Roth spots
(Moritz Roth, Swiss pathologist, 1839-1914)
The Roth spot, which occurs in infective endocarditis, is located in the retina and has the appearance of an exudate of cotton wool. It consists of aggregations of cytoid bodies. The association of these lesions with infective endocarditis was first recognized by Litten.

RSR pattern (rsr, rSr, RSr, RSR)
This pattern of the QRS complex is seen in lead V1 of the surface electrocardiogram in the presence of right bundle branch block.

Rubella syndrome
Infection of pregnant women with the rubella virus during the first trimester was one of the first events noted to have a reproducible effect on the developing heart. Cardiovascular disease occurs in about one-third of those infected at this crucial period of pregnancy, the commonest lesions produced being persistent patency of the arterial duct, septal defects and peripheral pulmonary arterial stenoses. The syndrome has largely been avoided by the expedient of immunizing girls before they reach child-bearing age.

Rudimentary ventricle
A ventricle which, in congenitally malformed hearts, lacks one or more of its component parts is said to be rudimentary and incomplete. Either the morphologically right or left ventricle can be malformed in this fashion. Usually the rudimentary ventricle lacks its inlet component, as seen with double inlet ventricle or absence of one atrioventricular connexion, or lacks its outlet component when there is double outlet from the other ventricle. More rarely, a rudimentary ventricle may lack

both inlet and outlet components. It is then simply a pouch composed of the apical trabecular component.
See *Ventricle*

RVH
see *Right ventricular hypertrophy*

Rytand's syndrome
(David Rytand, contemporary American cardiologist)
It is known that gross calcification of a diseased aortic valve can extend into the support mechanism of the valvar leaflets, involving the central fibrous body and membraneous septum. If the calcific process also involves the atrioventricular conduction axis, which is sandwiched between the membraneous septum and the crest of the ventricular septum, it can produce complete atrioventricular dissociation. This combination was first noted by Rytand and is known eponymously for him.

S

S wave
This wave is defined as that part of the surface electrocardiographic tracing of ventricular depolarization which is manifested as a negative deflection.

S_3 gallop
see *Third heart sound*

Saccular aneurysm
see *Aneurysm*

Sail sound in Ebstein's malformation
In the severest form of Ebstein's malformation, the anterosuperior leaflet of the tricuspid valve is tethered in linear fashion to an apical shelf within the right ventricle. As a consequence of the abnormal tethering, it flaps back and forth with each cardiac cycle, rather than opening and closing in normal fashion. The flapping produces a characteristic auscultatory sound which is known as the sail sound.

St Jude prosthesis
This mechanical prosthesis has two leaflets made of pyrolitic carbon. Haemodynamically, it is probably the best prosthetic valve yet devised and has a low incidence of thrombogenicity. It is currently used primarily for replacement of either the mitral or the aortic valve.

Salbutamol
Salbutamol is a beta$_2$ adrenoceptor agonist agent which can be administered orally, intravenously or by inhalation. Its haemodynamic effects are to increase myocardial contractility and heart rate, and reduce systemic vascular resistance. This haemodynamic profile means that its administration confers acute haemodynamic benefits to most patients with acute heart failure although, in some patients, myocardial ischaemia or arrhythmia may be precipitated.

Unfortunately, tolerance to the drug soon occurs and long term treatment of heart failure with salbutamol is normally counterproductive.

Salicylates
see *Aspirin*

Salt
Salt intake is thought to be of some importance in both hypertension and congestive heart failure. Studies have shown that diets high in sodium can, in genetically predisposed animals, produce hypertension. The role of sodium in the aetiology of hypertension in humans, however, has not been established. Some epidemiological studies have suggested a strong association between sodium and the prevalence of hypertension, but other factors, such as body weight, physical activity, and so on, complicate the assessment of this association. Restriction of sodium is beneficial for management of some patients with hypertension, but a recent study has shown that reduction of weight may be more important. Intake of salt is also of some importance in the management of patients with heart failure. Until recent years, restriction of the intake of salt was considered an integral part of the management of such patients, but the production of potent drugs, particularly diuretics and inhibitors of angiotensin converting enzyme, has lessened the importance of dietary advice in management.

Sandhoff's disease
see *Gangliosidoses*

Saphenous vein graft
One of the most popular conduits used to bypass coronary arterial atherosclerotic lesions during surgical treatment of ischaemic heart disease is the patient's own saphenous veins. The veins are harvested during the operative procedure and, when inserted between the aorta and the diseased coronary arteries, are positioned so that flow through them is the reverse of that during normal function. This is to obviate the presence of any valves that may exist within the segment used for the venous graft.

Sarcoidosis
Involvement of the heart in a patient with sarcoidosis is a serious complication. The effects are the result of granulomatous reactions within the myocardium, including the conduction tissues. Arrhythmias are a frequent presentation, and sudden death is by no means uncommon.

Sarcolemma
The sarcolemma is the distinct membrane which encases and delimits single cells of the myocardium. It is bounded on its outer aspect by the basal lamina. The sarcolemma is invaginated into the cell to produce the system of transverse tubules known as the T-system or T-tubules.

Sarcomere
The sarcomere is the functional subunit of the myofilaments of myocardial cell, in which the contractile elements interreact to produce shortening and lengthening of the cell. It is the part of an individual myofilament between two adjacent Z-lines (Figure 178).

Sarcoplasmic reticulum
The sarcoplasmic reticulum is a subcellular organelle made up of a fine network of tubules which surround the myofibrils, the individual tubules being orientated in the long axis of the myocardial cell. Unlike the system of T-tubules (which is derived from the sarcolemma), the sarcoplasmic reticulum is a closed system, and has no communication with the extracellular space. It is the equivalent of the endoplasmic reticulum found in other cells. The sarcoplasmic reticulum is

the site from which calcium ions are liberated to initiate cellular contraction.

Figure 178. Sarcomere. The sarcomere is that part of the myofilaments of myocardial cells between the two adjacent Z lines (arrows).

Sausage right ventricle
One of the rare congenital malformations which can involve the morphologically right ventricle is an absence of the ventricular apical component. As a result, the ventricle is, effectively, a smooth-walled tube joining the orifices of the tricuspid and pulmonary valves. When seen angiographically, the appearance is that of a sausage - hence the title sausage right ventricle. Should the abnormal ventricle become obstructive, treatment is by means of a Fontan procedure. Usually there is an accompanying atrial septal defect, and it may be necessary to close this communication surgically. See also *Hypoplasia of right ventricle*

Scheie's syndrome
This disease is one of the three manifestations of deficiency of alpha-L-iduronidase, the others being the Hurler syndrome and the intermediate syndrome (or Hurler-Scheie syndrome). Patients with the Scheie syndrome itself are less severely affected than those with Hurler syndrome. They have normal stature and intellect and a near normal life span. The most striking features are stiff joints and corneal clouding, while aortic stenosis and regurgitation or mitral regurgitation

are the principal cardiac findings. These are due to accumulation of heparan and dermatan sulphates in the tissues as a consequence of the enzymic deficiency. The cardiac lesions are managed as they would be in any otherwise normal individual. See also *Hurler syndrome: Hurler-Scheie syndrome*

Schistosomiasis
Schistosomiasis is a chronic disease found in tropical regions due to infection by any of three trematode worms; *Schistosoma mansoni, Schistosoma japonicum*, and *Schistosoma haematobium*. The life cycle of these worms is complicated. Eggs secreted in the urine or faeces of infected subjects pass into fresh water and hatch into ciliated miracidia which then penetrate into freshwater snails. They multiply in the snails and develop into free swimming larval form known as cercariae. Cercariae then penetrate the skin of swimming or bathing human subjects and pass, via the lungs and the liver, to the veins draining the intestines and urinary bladder. The mature worm remains in this position for many years, producing huge numbers of eggs, some of which are secreted in the urine and faeces, some are trapped locally causing fibrosis, and some are carried by the blood stream to the liver and the lungs. A heavy infection can cause blockage of the small pulmonary arterioles leading to pulmonary hypertension and, eventually, right heart failure.

Scimitar syndrome
Originally, this syndrome was described as the combination of a right-sided heart, sequestration of the lower lobe of the right lung and anomalous pulmonary arterial and venous connexions. The name is derived from the shadow produced on a chest radiograph by the anomalously connecting vein, which usually joins the inferior caval vein within the abdomen. The shadow was

thought to resemble the curved edge of a Turkish sword. It is now recognized that the syndrome can exist with various forms of expression, depending upon whether the bronchial, arterial and venous supplies of the abnormal lobe are collectively or individually abnormal. It is also known that the heart itself is not necessarily right-sided. Surgical treatment is needed in severly affected cases, which may necessitate lobectomy.

Scintigraphy
This technique involves the imaging of radiopharmaceuticals using a gamma camera. Mostly the term is used to refer to imaging of myocardial perfusion by thallium-201. See also *Myocardial perfusion imaging*

Scleroderma (progressive systemic sclerosis)
This insidious and chronic fibrosing condition presents as a progressive tightening and thickening of the skin which develops over a period of many years. Raynaud's phenomenon occurs at some time in almost all sufferers. Visceral involvement may occur at any time during the course of the disease, and affects the gastrointestinal tract, lungs, heart or kidney.
The importance of primary cardiac involvement in the natural history has been emphasized recently because involvement of the heart is a frequent cause of death. When the heart is affected, there is extensive intimal sclerosis of the small coronary arteries. Such involvement may lead to patchy ischaemia, small infarctions and ventricular myocardial fibrosis. The combination of vascular insufficiency and fibrosis produces a cardiomyopathic state with congestive heart failure and defects of the conduction system. Acute and chronic pericarditis are also well documented. Indeed, pericardial effusions can, at times, be large enough to cause tamponade and may require

pericardiocentesis or pericardiectomy. Many drugs have been used in treating the condition but without any significant or prolonged effect. The value of corticosteroids is limited to improvement of the early oedematous phase of the disease but their effect on the heart has yet to be systematically evaluated.

Sclerosis, arterial
see *Atherosclerosis*

Second heart sound
The second heart sound comprises two components, designated A2 and P2 respectively because they relate to closure of the aortic and pulmonary valves, the aortic preceding the pulmonary sound. The two components are usually best appreciated at the left sternal edge where an increase in their splitting can readily be elicited in association with inspiration. Wide splitting of the second sound with respiratory variation may occur in association with right bundle branch block or obstruction to the right ventricular outflow tract. Wide fixed splitting occurs in association with atrial septal defects. Paradoxical splitting occurs in association with left bundle branch block or obstruction of the left ventricular outflow tract.

Secondary dextrocardia
This arcane term is used to describe the situation in which the heart is right-sided in an otherwise normal individual as a consequence of some other disease process, such as a left-sided mass pushing the heart across the mediastinum or a right-sided pneumothorax drawing the heart across the midline. In these circumstances, it is far more sensible simply to describe the right-sided locality of the heart.

Secundum defects
Atrial septal defects occurring within the oval fossa are usually described as

Secundum defects

secundum defects, thus differentiating them from the so-called primum defect. In reality, the primum defect is an atrioventricular rather than an atrial septal defect, but one that permits only interatrial shunting. It is also important to know that the so-called secundum defects are due to a deficiency of the primary atrial septum, which forms the floor of the oval fossa. See also *Atrial septal defects: Ostium secundum defect: Oval fossa defect*

Segmental wall motion

This term refers to the motion of a limited portion of the ventricular surface. Abnormal motion may be described in terms of akinesia, hypokinesia or dyskinesia. It is usually associated with abnormalities (narrowings) of the coronary arterial tree.

Seldinger technique in cardiac catheterization

This technique is normally used for the introduction of cardiac catheters into the femoral artery so that the left heart may be entered via a retrograde approach. The artery is punctured by a needle following which a flexible tipped guide wire is introduced through the needle into the vessel. The needle is then removed, leaving the guide wire in position. The catheter is passed over the wire and, once the catheter is well into the artery, the guide wire is withdrawn leaving the catheter within the artery. The catheter can then be manoeuvred through the arterial system in order to investigate the left heart.

Selenium deficiency

Selenium is a trace element and an essential part of the enzyme glutathione peroxidase which functions to remove from cells organic hydroperoxidases. Deficiency or absence of the element produces a specific anomaly known as Keshan disease. The disease was recognized in extensive areas of China

where the content of selenium in food and soil is very low. The effect on the heart is to produce a cardiomyopathy which, once fully developed, is irreversible. The incidence of the disease has now been significantly reduced by providing dietary supplements of selenium.

Semilunar valve

The arterial valves (aortic, pulmonary and truncal) are also known as semilunar valves because of the likeness of the valvar leaflets to the halfmoon (Figure 179). It is, in fact, the individual leaflets rather than the overall valve, which are semilunar.

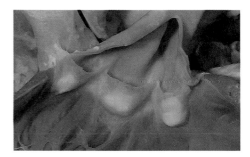

Figure 179. Semilunar valves. This picture of the pulmonary valve shows how each individual leaflet is shaped like a half-moon.

Senning procedure

(Ake Senning, Swedish surgeon now domiciled in Switzerland)
The earliest successful technique devised to reverse surgically the atrial venous connexions in patients with complete transposition was performed by Senning. An ingenious procedure, it employed the existing atrial tissues rearranged by careful incisions and sutures to connect the caval veins to the mitral valve and the pulmonary veins to the tricuspid valve. The procedure, at first sight, is difficult to understand and perform. It was overtaken by the Mustard procedure as the atrial redirection procedure of

choice during the 1970s, but recently the Senning operation has achieved a renaissance, since it is thought less likely to produce the problems of venous obstruction which have plagued the Mustard procedure. Both operations, nonetheless, carry a high risk of postoperative arrhythmias, and both call upon the morphologically right ventricle to perform an unnatural role in supporting the systemic circulation (as a consequence of the discordant ventriculoarterial connexion). The most recent surgical trend, therefore, is to perform arterial redirection procedures rather than either the Senning or Mustard operations. If atrial redirection is required, then either of the two options has its strong advocates and detractors. See also *Arterial switch: Complete transposition: Mustard procedure*

Septal band
see *Septomarginal trabeculation*

Septal defects
One of the commonest types of congenital malformation is a hole between the cardiac chambers or great arteries. This group of lesions collectively is known as septal defects, although the holes present are often outside the confines of the normal septal structures. The defects may involve the atrial, atrioventricular, ventricular or aortopulmonary septal structures. Each is defined and amplified under the appropriate heading.

Septal myotomy-myectomy
This procedure is the incision and/or resection of septal tissue from the left ventricle in patients with hypertrophic cardiomyopathy. The procedure must be performed with care, since the left bundle branch cascades down the left ventricular aspect of the septum. Myotomy or myectomy, however, can be performed without damaging these tissues.

Septal rupture
Rupture of the myocardium is the second most frequent cause of pump failure in patients with myocardial infarction, accounting for about one-fifth of deaths in the acute phase. The rupture can involve either the free wall or the septum. Septal rupture occurs more frequently with anterior than with inferior infarcts, and usually when the infarction itself is extensive. Rupture leads to overload of both ventricles, but right ventricular failure is exacerbated when the process also affects the papillary muscles of the tricuspid valve. Once diagnosis is obtained, (now readily achieved with cross-sectional echocardiography) treatment is surgical. However, very recently, post-infarction ruptures have been closed by umbrellas inserted via catheters.

Septal thickening
Thickening of the ventricular septum usually occurs with hypertrophic cardiomyopathy, when it tends to bulge into and block the left ventricular outflow tract. Septal thickening can also be the consequence of storage disorders.

Septomarginal trabeculation
This term was initially introduced by Tandler in 1913 to describe the extensive septal muscular structures within the morphologically right ventricle. One of these extended from the septum to the anterior papillary muscle of the tricuspid valve, and it is this structure (the moderator band) which is defined as the septomarginal trabeculation in the Nomina Anatomica. Tandler, however, also used the term to describe the more extensive complex of which the moderator band is but a part, and it is in this latter context that the term is used in modern day paediatric cardiology, being a synonym for the septal band. As thus defined, the trabeculation has a body which reinforces the septal surface of the right ventricle, anterior

Septomarginal trabeculation

and posterior limbs which diverge to clasp the supraventricular crest, and a leash of apical extensions, one of which is the moderator band. The septomarginal trabeculation also supports much of the tension apparatus of the tricuspid valve, including the medial and anterior papillary muscles.

Septoparietal trabeculations
A series of smaller muscular trabeculations are found in the normal right ventricle extending from the anterocephalic border of the septomarginal trabeculation and running onto the parietal wall of the ventricle (Figure 180). These are described as the septoparietal trabeculations. They are usually grossly hypertrophied in tetralogy of Fallot, producing much of the muscular subpulmonary obstruction.

Septostomy
Septostomy describes the iatrogenic rupturing of a septal structure, almost always the atrial septum. Nowadays, it is usually done with a balloon (the Rashkind septostomy), but can be achieved by means of a blade inserted via a catheter or at surgery. See also *Blade atrial septostomy: Rashkind procedure*

Septum
A septal structure is any part of the heart which separates two adjacent structures. Thus, within the heart, it is conventional to describe the atrial, ventricular and atrioventricular septal structures, whereas the arterial trunks are septated by the aortopulmonary septum. The ventricular septum is itself described in terms of its constituent parts (inlet, trabecular, outlet septal structures). A septum is also described within a chamber, such as the sinus septum between the orifice of the coronary sinus and the oval fossa.

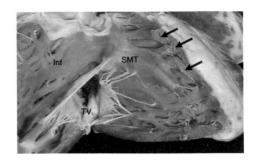

Figure 180. Septoparietal trabeculations. This view of the opened right ventricle shows the septoparietal trabeculations (arrowed) extending from the anterior margin of the septomarginal trabeculation (SMT). (TV – tricuspid valve; Inf infundibulum)

Sequential segmental analysis
This logical system of analysis is now widely employed to bring rigour into the diagnosis and description of congenitally malformed hearts. In essence, the system is based upon the principle that all malformed hearts have three basic segments, atria, ventricles and arterial trunks, and that there are very limited ways in which these segments can be anatomically arranged and connected to one another. If analysis always commences with a breakdown of the segmental arrangements and interconnexions, it is then an easy matter to catalogue any and all associated malformations within the heart, and to analyze the overall cardiac structure in terms of the basic arrangement of the body. Thus, sequential segmental analysis starts with the determination of atrial arrangement, this being based upon the structure of the appendages. Thereafter, the arrangement of the ventricular mass is ascertained according to the morphology and relationships of the ventricles, be they normal or abnormal. The nature of the atrioventricular junction is then determined in respect of connexion of adjacent chambers and the morphology of the atrioventricular valves.

A similar process at the ventriculoarterial junction accounts for the pattern of the arterial trunks, the nature of their connexion to the ventricular mass and the morphology of the arterial valves. Associated malformations are then catalogued sequentially, starting at the venoatrial junctions and progressing through to the aortic and pulmonary pathways. Finally, the position of the heart and the location of its apex is recorded and, when appropriate, a full catalogue is made of the arrangement of the abdominal and thoracic organs. In this way, normality is always proved rather than assumed.

Serotonin
see *5-Hydroxytryptamine*

Serum cardiac enzymes
Measurement of cardiac enzymes is used in the diagnosis of myocardial infarction. Myocardial cells, when injured irreversibly, are known to release a number of enzymes into the circulation where their levels can be measured using specific chemical reactions. The three enzymes most commonly measured are creatinine phosphokinase, glutamic-oxyloacetic transferase and lactic dehydrogenase. Following myocardial damage, the release of these enzymes peaks at differing times. Activity of creatinine phosphokinase within the serum exceeds the normal range within six to eight hours following the onset of infarction, peaks at 24 hours and declines to normal within three to four days after the onset of chest pain. Activity of glutamic-oxyloacetic transferase exceeds the normal range within 8-12 hours following the onset of pain, peaks at 18-36 hours and falls to normal within three to four days. Levels of lactic dehydrogenase rise and fall more slowly than the other two enzymes and usually only exceed the normal range from one to two days after the onset of pain. Activity peaks at three to six days, while

levels may be elevated for up to 14 days following infarction.
All three enzymes are found not only in myocardial tissues but also in other tissues. An elevation of enzymes may, therefore, to some extent, be non-specific. This problem has been countered by the measurement of specific isoenzymes, particularly the isoenzyme of creatinine phosphokinase. This isoenzyme is measured by a radioimmunoassay technique and is, at present, the most sensitive marker for assessing myocardial damage.

Sheffield protocol
This protocol, first proposed in 1972, involves progressive graded exercise on a treadmill and is used in the diagnosis of coronary arterial disease. In reality, the Sheffield protocol is a variant of the Bruce protocol with the addition of two preliminary stages, each of three minutes' duration. In these two stages, the patient walks at the same speed (1.7 mph) as in the first grade of the Bruce protocol, but with a treadmill gradient of zero and then 5%.

Shock
Shock is a non-specific term. It describes the condition characterized by a fall in blood pressure and the subsequent poor blood flow to all the tissues of the body. This reduction in flow of blood usually results in pallor and sweating, with cold limbs, restlessness and oliguria. Tachycardia is usually a secondary phenomenon. In a cardiological context, cardiogenic shock is normally a complication of massive myocardial infarction and carries a high mortality - usually in the region of 30-40%. Treatment is by a combination of vasopressor agents and/or use of the intra-aortic balloon pump.

Shoulder hand syndrome
This condition of unknown aetiology is a rare late complication of acute

myocardial infarction. It is characterized by pain, stiffness and limitation of movement of the shoulder and hand joints together with oedema and, ultimately, atrophy of the subcutaneous tissues. Normally, scintigraphy of bones using technetium-99 shows an increased uptake of tracer, most notably in the periarticular regions. Nearly always the condition is self-limiting but physiotherapy seems to be effective in hastening its resolution.

Shunt

In cardiological terms, shunting represents an abnormal communication between the systemic and pulmonary sides of the circulations. The shunt may be from left-to-right as occurs, for example, in uncomplicated atrial septal defects, ventricular septal defects, or patency of the arterial duct. Alternatively, it may be right-to-left, as occurs when these defects are associated with pulmonary hypertension, the pulmonary blood pressure exceeding the systemic blood pressure. These shunts may also be bidirectional at different phases of the cardiac cycle. A third type of shunt seen in cardiological practice is that found in association with arteriovenous malformations, where there is direct shunting from the arterial to the venous circulation which bypasses the network of capillaries. Such malformations may occur either in the lungs or in the peripheral circulation. See also *Arteriovenous malformations: Atrial septal defects: Patency of arterial duct: Ventricular septal defect*

Shy-Drager syndrome

(George Milton Shy, U.S. physician, 1919-1967; Glenn Albert Drager, U.S. neurologist, born 1917)
The Shy-Drager syndrome, first described in 1960, is the name given to the clinical picture of progressive autonomic failure with urinary incontinence, impotence, loss of sweating and postural hypotension, often also associated with akinesia and rigidity. The disease is unremitting and death normally occurs five to ten years after the onset of symptoms. Treatment is imperfect but fludrocortisone, monoamine oxidase inhibitors (by augmenting noradrenaline concentrations in nerve endings), indomethacin (by inhibiting the production of vasodilatory prostaglandins), elastic stockings or the wearing of an antigravity suit (such as worn by astronauts) may help to relieve the symptoms partially.

Sick sinus syndrome

This syndrome is described when there are electrocardiographic criteria which provide evidence of sinus nodal dysfunction. Typically, the syndrome is characterized by cerebral or cardiac dysfunction in association with sinus bradycardia, sinus arrest, sinuatrial block, tachyarrhythmias, carotid sinus hypersensitivity or any combination of these.

Signal-averaging techniques

This technique involves the application of the signal averaging process to increase the amplitude of small signals which bear a constant relationship to a fixed trigger point in the electrocardiogram, but which are not evident on standard recordings because of background noise. High amplification and superimposition of numerous complexes allows the signal of interest to be enhanced while random noise is cancelled out.

Silent ischaemia

This term is used to describe an episode in whch a patient exhibits the electrocardiographic changes of myocardial ischaemia (ST segment depression) but does not experience, during the episode, the symptoms of angina pectoris. Such silent ischaemia can be identified either by analysis of the ST segments of 24 hour ambulatory electrocardiographic recordings or by exercise stress testing, and occurs in approximately 40% of patients with coronary arterial disease. Subjects exhibiting silent ischaemia have an increased incidence of coronary events and a worse prognosis than patients in whom myocardial ischaemia is associated with the symptom of angina pectoris.

Simpson's rule

This method is a way of calculating left ventricular volume which avoids the use of geometric assumptions and which can therefore be used even when the ventricular shape is markedly distorted. The method depends on dividing, or slicing, the ventricular cavity into a series of ellipsoid cylinders. The sum of the volumes of the individual slices then gives the total ventricular volume. The greater the number of slices employed, the greater the accuracy of the method. Mathematically, the method can be expressed by the following formula:

$$V = \frac{\pi}{4} (H) \sum_{0}^{n} (D1)(D2)$$

where V is the total volume; H is the height of the individual slices; D1 and D2 are the orthogonal short axis diameters of the slices and n is the number of slices.

The limitation of the method is the practical difficulty of obtaining multiple slices and the mathematical complexity of the calculation.

Single gene disorders

A gene, or allele, is a piece of DNA which includes the code for a single polypeptide chain. These genes are carried on the molecule of DNA contained within each chromosome. For example, it is known that the smallest recognizable band on chromosome 1 carries enough DNA for 2000 – 3000 genes. If it can be shown that an abnormality in one pair of genes produces a malformation of the heart, then that anomaly is known as a single gene disorder. The defect obeys the basic Mendelian rules of inheritance, and will express itself in autosomal dominant or recessive fashion, or will be linked to the sex chromosomes (X-linked). An example of an autosomal recessive disorder affecting the heart is Pompe's disease, while Marfan's syndrome is a single gene disorder expressing itself in autosomal dominant fashion, as is Noonan's syndrome. Duchenne muscular dystrophy is a typical example of an X-linked disorder. Several hundred syndromes, many involving the heart, have now been recognized as single gene disorders, but these still account for very much the minority of congenital heart malformations as a whole.

Single outlet ventriculoarterial connexion

When only a solitary arterial trunk can be traced from its origin at the base of the heart, there is said to be single outlet from the heart. Most frequently the solitary trunk is also a common trunk, supplying directly the pulmonary, systemic and coronary arterial circulations. Less frequently, one arterial trunk may be atretic, yet its cardiac origin cannot be identified with certainty. In these circumstances, the connexion is again defined as a variant of single outlet, either a solitary aortic trunk with pulmonary atresia, or a solitary pulmonary trunk with aortic atresia. Less frequently, there may be complete absence of the pulmonary trunk. In this setting, there is no certainty as to whether the arterial trunk is an aorta or a common trunk. It is most accurately described simply as a solitary arterial trunk (Figure 181).

Single photon emission computed tomography

This technique is a form of tomographic imaging of a radiopharmaceutical using

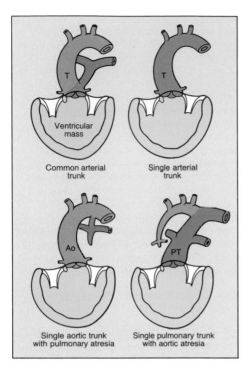

Figure 181. Single outlet ventriculoarterial connexion. These diagrams show the morphological patterns of the ventriculoarterial connexions fulfilling the criteria for single outlet from the ventricle. (T – common arterial trunk; Ao – aorta; PT – pulmonary trunk)

a gamma camera. The commonest form uses a rotating camera to acquire images from many angles around the patient and the tomograms are then reconstructed from these. Initial reconstruction is of slices perpendicular to the axis of rotation, but oblique slices can be reconstructed from a stack of transaxial slices. When applied to the imaging of thallium-201, the precision and ease of interpretation is much greater than for conventional planar imaging and permit the three dimensional distribution of myocardial perfusion to be assessed. See also *Computed axial tomography: Myocardial perfusion imaging: Thallium-201*

Single ventricle

This term has probably been responsible for as much confusion as any other used in the vocabulary of congenital heart disease. Logically, the term would describe a heart with a solitary ventricular chamber and, rarely, hearts do exist with this morphologic arrangement (Figure 182). In the past, however, the condition was defined in terms of a double inlet atrioventricular connexion, and it became conventional to describe all hearts with double inlet ventricle as 'single ventricle'. The problem with this approach is that almost all hearts with this connexion have two ventricles, albeit that one is large and dominant and the other is small, rudimentary and incomplete. Various artificial systems were designed to circumvent the illogicalities produced by this convention, but none were satisfactory. All the difficulties are removed by the simple expedient of describing hearts with double inlet ventricle for what they are, for example, double inlet left ventricle and so on. Hearts with solitary ventricles can then sensibly be described as having 'single ventricles' without fear of producing confusion.

Sinuatrial block

This type of conduction block occurs when there is interruption of normal conduction between the sinus node and the surrounding atrial myocardium. The site of block may be within the sinus node itself or within the sinuatrial junction. *First degree sinuatrial block* occurs when there is an abnormally prolonged sinuatrial conduction time. This cannot be recognized on the surface electrocardiogram. *Second degree block* is characterized by a periodic failure of the sinus impulse to propagate to the atrium. It is manifested as periodic absence

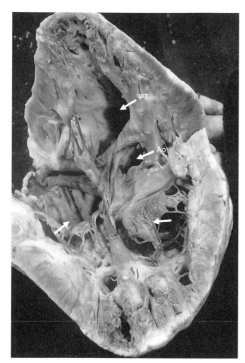

Figure 182. Single ventricle. In this rare congenitally malformed heart, a solitary ventricle receives both atrioventricular valves (arrowed) and gives rise to both arterial trunks. (Ao – aorta; PT – pulmonary trunk)

of the P wave. Sinuatrial Wenckebach periodicity will be evident when there is progressive shortening of the PP interval prior to the dropped P wave. *Advanced second degree sinuatrial block* exists when there is regular interruption of P waves. In this setting, the pause between P waves will be an exact multiple of the normal PP interval. *Third degree block* occurs when there is complete interruption between discharge of sinus impulses and the surrounding atrium.

Sinuatrial conduction time
This is the time taken for an impulse to be conducted across the sinuatrial junction.

Sinuatrial disease
Any abnormality of formation of the impulse within the sinus node, or its conduction through the sinus node and the sinuatrial junction, is described as sinuatrial disease.

Sinuatrial exit block
see *Sinuatrial block*

Sinuatrial node
see *Sinus node*

Sinus arrest
This occurs when there is cessation of formation of the impulse within the sinus node (Figure 183). Characteristically, the arrest does not constitute an exact multiple of the normal PP interval, thus allowing its distinction from sinuatrial block.

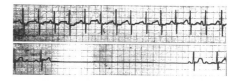

Figure 183. Sinus arrest. Following termination of atrial tachycardia in this patient with disease of the sinus node, there is an eight second episode of sinus arrest.

Sinus arrhythmia
This irregularity of cardiac rhythm occurs when each beat originates within the sinus node. A clear definition of sinus arrhythmia has not been established. Some consider it to be present when the difference between the shortest and longest PP interval is greater than 120 ms. Others include variations in length of the sinus cycle of 10% or more together with variations in PP intervals of 160 ms or greater. A degree of sinus arrhythmia is normally present following the phases of respiration. Sinus arrhythmia is also often present in second and third

degree atrioventricular block, so-called ventricular phasic sinus arrhythmia.

Sinus bradycardia
This pattern is seen when a rhythm originating within the sinus node has a rate of less than 60 beats per minute (Figure 184).

V5

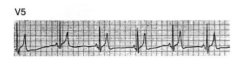

Figure 184. Sinus bradycardia. This rhythm strip (lead V5) shows marked bradycardia of sinus origin at a rate of 40 beats per minute.

Sinus of Morgagni
see *Aortic sinus*

Sinus nodal artery
The artery to the sinus node is the largest of the atrial arteries. In 55% of individuals it is a branch of the right coronary artery, arising from the circumflex artery in the remainder although, in a small proportion of cases, the artery may arise directly from one or other aortic sinus. In almost all instances, the artery arises from the proximal part of the stem artery and courses through the interatrial groove towards the superior cavoatrial junction. In an important minority, the artery may originate more distally and cross either the right atrial appendage or the dome of the left atrium to reach the sinus node in the terminal groove of the right atrium. The artery may enter the groove itself by passing in front of or behind the cavoatrial junction, or else may divide and form a circle around the junction. The node itself it usually arranged around the prominent nodal artery.

Sinus nodal re-entry
This is a re-entrant tachycardia which originates in the region of the sinus node. It is characteristically paroxysmal, with either no change in P wave morphology from normal sinus beats or very minor alterations. Its rate is usually between 100 and 140 beats a minute.

Sinus node
The sinus node, or pacemaker of the heart, is a small cigar-shaped conglomeration of specialized myocardial tissue lying at the junction of the superior caval vein with the morphologically right atrium (Figure 185). The node is usually found lateral to the cavoatrial junction, but may, in one-tenth of individuals, be disposed in horseshoe fashion across the crest of the atrial appendage. It is made up of small, interweaving cells set in a dense fibrous matrix and, usually, is arranged around the prominent nodal artery. At its margins, the nodal cells are distinct from the atrial myocardium, with only short transitional zones. The node is duplicated in hearts with isomerism of the right atrial appendages and, conversely, poorly formed or absent when there is isomerism of the morphologically left appendages.

Sinus node arrest
This is the same as sinus arrest. It is due to cessation of formation of the impulse within the node. The fact that the period of arrest is not an exact multiple of the normal PP interval permits its distinction from sinuatrial block.

Sinus node disease
see *Sick sinus syndrome*

Sinus of pericardium
The pericardial cavity is, in effect, formed between the thick fibrous pericardium and the epicardium. Within this overall space, there are two recesses or sinuses lined by serous pericardium.

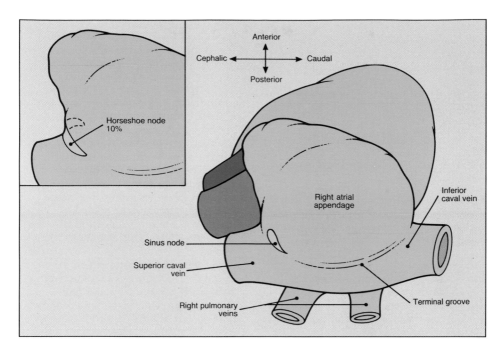

Figure 185. Sinus node. This diagram, drawn in surgical orientation, shows the usual position of the sinus node and its 'horse-shoe' variation which is found in 10% of cases.

One, between the back of the arterial pedicle and the front of the atria, is the transverse sinus. The other, a recess between the pulmonary veins and the inferior caval veins, is the oblique sinus. See also *Pericardium*

Sinus pause
This describes a transient cessation of automaticity of the sinus node and, hence, is synonymous with sinus arrest. Sinus pause, however, by implication, indicates a brief cessation of nodal activity while arrest of the node may be prolonged.

Sinus rhythm
This is the normal cardiac rhythm which at rest has a rate in adults which is arbitrarily defined as being

between 60 and 100 beats per minute. The sinus nature of such a rhythm, however, can only be established electrocardiographically when atrial depolarization is seen to result from discharge of the sinus node. The P wave will be upright in leads I, II and aVF negative in aVR, and will have a frontal axis of 0°– 90°(Figure 186).

Sinus septum
This term describes the part of the musculature of the morphologically right atrium which separates the orifice of the coronary sinus from the floor of the oval fossa (fossa ovalis). The tendon of Todaro runs through the septum to embed itself within the central fibrous body, thus forming one of the important boundaries of the triangle of Koch. See also *Koch's triangle: Tendon of Todaro*

Sinus tachycardia
This describes a discharge rate from the sinus node which is greater than

315

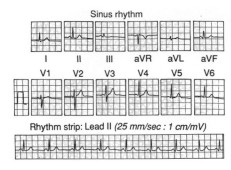

Rhythm strip: Lead II *(25 mm/sec : 1 cm/mV)*

Figure 186. Sinus rhythm. The normal frontal P wave axis (+60°) and the upright P waves in the chest leads indicate that the rhythm is sinus in origin.

100 beats per minute, but usually no more than 180 beats per minute in the adult. Such tachycardia generally has a gradual onset and offset. It is the normal response to a variety of physiological or pathophysiological stresses.

Sinus of Valsalva
see *Aortic sinus*

Sinus venosus
The endocardial tube of the developing heart is conventionally divided into five segments. The most proximal of these, forming the junction between the heart and the veins developing within the embryo, yolk sac, and placenta is called the sinus venosus. Initially a bilaterally symmetrical structure, the sinus is remodelled extensively during development and, eventually, is incorporated almost exclusively within the venous sinus of the morphologically right atrium.

Sinus venosus defect
This particular type of interatrial communication exists when either the superior (usual) or inferior (rare) caval vein has a connexion to both the right and left atrial chambers. Almost always there is associated anomalous connexion of the right pulmonary veins at the cavoatrial junction. The lesion makes up about 10% of all interatrial communications and presents in the same fashion as a septal defect within the oval fossa. The distinction from the oval fossa defect is difficult to make echocardiographically, but is readily evident angiographically. Surgical repair is needed, and care must be taken to reroute the systemic and pulmonary venous pathways without damaging the sinus node or its artery. The name sinus venosus defect was coined by Ross in 1956, but any connexion with the embryonic venous sinus is remote.

Sinuventricular conduction
In certain rare circumstances, such as experimental conditions under high concentrations of potassium, an impulse can be shown to pass from the sinus to the atrioventricular nodes without any evidence of involvement of the working atrial myocardium. This circumstance can also be encountered in clinical practice, where there is atrial conduction without any electrocardiographic evidence of atrial contraction. The phenomenon, known as sinuventricular conduction, is cited as one of the strongest pieces of evidence in favour of an internodal atrial conduction system. As yet, however, no one has shown that the cells responsible for the sinuventricular conduction are any different morphologically from the rest of the atrial myocardium.

Situs
This Greek word means, quite simply, arrangement. It is used in cardiological terminology to describe the pattern of structures, such as the organs or the atria.

Situs ambiguus
It is the overall jumbled-up arrangement of the abdominal organs in patients with visceral heterotaxy ('splenic

syndromes') which attracted the title of situs ambiguus. When the thoracic organs or atria are analysed in logical fashion in patients with this arrangement, nonetheless, they are found to show symmetry of formation rather than demonstrating any ambiguity. The arrangement in the chest, therefore, is better described in terms of right or left isomerism (of the lungs, bronchi or atrial appendages) rather than 'situs ambiguus'.

Situs inversus
In the so-called inverted arrangement of the organs, all the anticipated right-sided structures are found on the left side of the body and vice-versa. The inversion is, therefore, a mirror-image arrangement and is by far the rarest form of body template.

Situs solitus
Solitus simply means usual, hence the term means usual arrangement of the organs. Such an arrangement, including the heart, is found in the overwhelming majority of patients with acquired heart disease, and in almost all those with congenital cardiac malformations.

Figure 187. Skeleton of heart. This illustration was prepared by removing, by dissection, the leaflets of the mitral (MV), aortic (AoV) and tricuspid (TV) valves from the heart. The fibrous skeleton is best formed at the central fibrous body (arrowed), where the leaflets of all three valves are in fibrous continuity.

Skeleton of heart
The fibrous skeleton of the heart serves two functions. First, it anchors the leaflets of the cardiac valves and secures them to the ventricular myocardium. Second, it insulates electrically the atrial from the ventricular myocardial masses except at the point of penetration of the atrioventricular conduction axis. Although often illustrated as complete rings supporting the leaflets of all four valves, such a concept of the cardiac skeleton is simplistic and unsupported by anatomic facts. The skeleton is best formed at the central fibrous body, where the leaflets of the mitral, tricuspid and aortic valves are in continuity (Figure 187). Apart from this area, the skeleton is variably formed, offering only limited support to the tricuspid valve and none to the leaflets of the pulmonary valve.

Smoking
Cigarette smoking is an independent risk factor for the development of coronary artery disease. The absolute risk is related to the length of time the subject has been smoking and the number of cigarettes smoked per day. Fortunately, if a person gives up smoking, the risk of developing coronary arterial disease reverts within two years to almost the same level as someone who has never smoked. In patients with established coronary arterial disease, a smoking habit is associated with an increased incidence of myocardial infarction and sudden death. Subjects who continue to smoke following myocardial infarction, or coronary artery bypass surgery, have a worse prognosis than those who discontinue the habit. The means by which smoking causes coronary arterial disease are not fully understood. Several mechanisms have been postulated, including accelerated atherosclerosis due to systemic hypertension, smoking-induced reduction in serum levels of high density lipoproteins, and damage to arterial epithelium by circulating carbon

monoxide and by nicotine-induced platelet agglutination.

Snowman silhouette
see *Cardiac silhouette: Totally anomalous pulmonary venous connexion*

Sodium nitrite
see *Nitrates and nitrites*

Sodium nitroprusside
see *Nitroprusside*

Sodium potassium pump
All surface membranes of cells have pumps for transport of sodium and potassium which require adenosine triphosphate for their activity. The pumps work to maintain intracellular homeostasis by pumping sodium out of and potassium into the cell.

Soldier's heart
see *DaCosta syndrome*

Solitary aortic trunk with pulmonary atresia
In some congenitally malformed hearts in which there is atresia of the pulmonary outflow tract, it is not always possible with certainty to ascertain the origin of the atretic pulmonary trunk. If this origin can be determined, the ventriculoarterial connexion is described as the case may be, for example, a discordant or double outlet connexion with pulmonary atresia. When, however, it is not possible to determine accurately the origin of the pulmonary trunk, the connexion cannot be described accurately in this fashion. Instead, the connexion is described in terms of a solitary aorta with pulmonary atresia, specifying separately the precise ventricular origin of the aorta (from right ventricle, left ventricle, or overriding). This connexion is then one variant of single outlet of the heart. See also *Single outlet ventriculo-arterial connexion*

Solitary arterial trunk
A solitary arterial trunk, as opposed to a solitary aorta, is described in those situations where the pulmonary trunk is completely absent. In these circumstances, it cannot be determined whether the solitary trunk is aortic or, initially, common. Hence the simple designation of solitary trunk.

Solitary pulmonary trunk with aortic atresia
This ventriculoarterial connexion is the counterpart of a solitary aorta with pulmonary atresia, except that the variant with aortic atresia is much rarer. When there is an atretic subaortic outflow tract, it is almost always possible to trace the ventricular origin of the hypoplastic aorta as, for example, in the hypoplastic left heart syndrome, where the ventriculo-arterial connexion is concordant. In those very rare examples when the ventricular origin of the aorta cannot be traced, then the connexion is catalogued as the variant of single outlet with a solitary pulmonary trunk and aortic atresia. It is also necessary to state precisely the ventricular origin of the pulmonary trunk. See also *Single outlet ventriculoarterial connexion*

Sones catheter
This catheter was designed by Mason Sones. It is introduced into the arterial circulation using the transbrachial approach. One advantage of the Sones catheter is that it can be used both for selective coronary arteriography and for left ventricular angiography. It is not ideal, however, for either of these procedures. Because of this, many cardiac laboratories have now switched to using other catheter designs.

Sones technique
This is the name given to the technique of selective coronary arteriography when the circulation is approached by way of a brachial arteriotomy. The method

was first described by Mason Sones in 1959. In properly trained and experienced hands, the technique is swift and safe with an incidence of complications comparable to that of the more widely used Judkins technique.

Sotalol
Sotalol is a non-selective beta-adrenoceptor antagonist agent. Because it has low lipid solubility, sotalol does not easily cross the blood-brain barrier and, therefore, it can be used in those subjects who suffer central nervous system side-effects when treated with highly lipid soluble beta-blocker agents such as propranolol. The novel feature of sotalol is that, in addition to possessing class 2 antiarrhythmic activity, it also has class 3 activity, prolonging the duration of the action potential. Its antiarrhythmic role in clinical practice has been intensively investigated and it has been shown to be as effective as amiodarone in the control of ventricular arrhythmias.

Sounds
Sounds, usually of diagnostic value, represent many different kinds. They are described throughout under their names, for instance, Korotkoff, second, third and fourth. Heart sounds are heard on auscultation and correspond to events in the cardiac cycle.

Spasm
see *Prinzmetal angina*

Sphingolipidoses
This group of diseases is characterized by inborn abnormalities of lipid metabolism. There are three main variants within the group. Niemann-Pick disease is the consequence of deficiency of sphingomyelinase. The heart is not usually affected. Gaucher's disease is due to excessive accumulation of glucosylceramide within the reticuloendothelial system. Cardiac

involvement is usually secondary to involvement of the lungs although, rarely, there may be direct infiltration of the myocardium or pericardium. The heart, however, is a major target in the third variant, Fabry's disease. This is due to deficiency of alpha-galactosidase-A which results in accumulation of phosphosphingolipids in the myocardium, conduction tissues, and valvar leaflets. The disease is X-linked, with the locus for the enzyme involved being on the long arm of the X-chromosome. The major cardiac manifestations are conduction disturbances, myocardial thickening and ischaemia as a consequence of involvement of the coronary vessels. The disease is progressive and, in male homozygotes, usually results in death during early adult life. The heterozygotic female, in contrast, suffers few problems. Prenatal diagnosis is now available but, other that this, treatment can only be supportive although enzymic replacement therapy may be feasible in the near future. See also *Fabry's disease: Gaucher's disease*

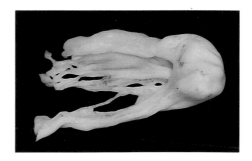

Figure 188. Spinnaker syndrome. This windsock-like extension of the Eustachian valve was removed at surgery from a patient in whom it was producing tricuspid obstruction.

Spinnaker syndrome
In rare circumstances, the valves of the inferior caval vein and coronary sinus

(Eustachian and Thebesian valves) may be unduly prominent as a congenital malformation. They may then become aneurysmally dilated and extend as a windsock-like structure through the tricuspid valve, blocking the right atrioventricular orifice or producing subpulmonary obstruction (Figure 188). Once diagnosed, which is now relatively easy with cross-sectional echocardiography, the obstructive lesion can be surgically removed. This combination is also called the spinnaker syndrome, since the lesion can be likened to a spinnaker sail. Rarely, the lesion may be derived from the leaflets of the tricuspid valve or from an aneurysmally dilated membranous sinus rather than the venous valves of the right atrium.

Spinothalamic evoked potentials
These are electrical signals which result from neuronal activity in the spinothalamic tracts of the spinal cord. Recognition of their presence confirms the functional integrity of the spinal cord. One of the major complications of surgery involving the thoracic aorta is paraplegia which results from impairment of the blood supply to the spinal cord. Monitoring for the presence of evoked spinothalamic potentials during this sort of surgery, therefore, adds to the safety of the procedure, since their disappearance indicates that the supply of blood to the cord is compromised and that immediate corrective action is required.

Spironolactone
Spironolactone is a drug which acts as a direct competitive inhibitor of aldosterone. Its effectiveness is governed by the serum concentration of this hormone. Aldosterone acts on the cells in the distal convoluted tubules of the kidneys, promoting absorption of salt in exchange for potassium. Spironolactone thus has a diuretic effect by preventing salt (and, therefore, water)

reabsorption in the distal convoluted tubule. Because spironolactone increases the concentration of potassium in the serum, it is normally given in conjunction with a potassium-losing loop diuretic.

Splenic syndromes
It is known that, amongst those with the most severely congenitally malformed hearts, there is a group of patients with associated abnormal location of the abdominal organs, almost always with malformations of the spleen, and collectively known as visceral heterotaxy, or as the splenic syndromes. It is now established, however, that the hallmark of the hearts themselves in these syndromes is the presence of isomerism of the atrial appendages. Furthermore, in almost all cases, the thoracic organs are also arranged in isomeric fashion. The splenic anomalies are less constant but, in most cases, absence of the spleen (asplenia) goes along with isomerism of the right appendages while an isomeric pattern of the left appendages is almost always accompanied by multiple spleens (polysplenia). See also *Isomerism*

Splinter haemorrhages
Splinter haemorrhages are associated with infective endocarditis. They are slightly raised, non-tender, haemorrhagic lesions that occur under the nail beds. They are thought to be autoimmune in nature.

Splitting of heart sounds
see *Fourth heart sound: Second heart sound: Third heart sound*

Spontaneous diastolic depolarization
This characteristic is possessed by pacemaker cells, particularly of the sinus and atrioventricular nodes, whereby the resting potential does not remain constant in diastole but gradually depolarizes. If a propagating impulse does not depolarize the pacemaker cell, it will reach a threshold and spontaneously

develop an action potential. The slope of such spontaneous depolarization (also called phase 4 of the action potential) is greatest in the cell of the sinus node. The slope is less further distally in the conduction system (with the result that the sinus rate normally predominates). The ionic basis for the depolarization is believed to be the inward sodium current.

Square root sign in constrictive pericarditis

A number of characteristic features of constrictive pericarditis can be recorded on pressure traces taken at cardiac catheterization. There is elevation and virtual identity of right atrial, right ventricular diastolic, left atrial and left ventricular diastolic traces. The right and left ventricular diastolic pressure traces also show an early diastolic dip followed by a pressure plateau. This shape is similar to the square root sign as used in mathematics, and the term has become associated with this condition.

Squatting

The adoption of a squatting posture following exertion is a feature commonly found in children with cyanotic congenital heart disease, most characteristically in those children with Fallot's tetralogy. The action of squatting increases systemic venous return and raises systemic vascular resistance and, therefore, systemic arterial pressure. The rise in arterial pressure and, hence, left ventricular pressure tends to improve systemic arterial oxygen saturation by reducing right to left shunting at ventricular level. The increased systemic venous return may also increase pulmonary blood flow. Asking a patient to squat can also be used as a diagnostic manoeuvre when auscultating the heart. For instance, in hypertrophic obstructive cardiomyopathy the increase in arterial pressure produced by squatting causes an increase in left ventricular end systolic

volume. This leads to a reduction in the gradient across the outflow tract and a consequent diminution in the intensity of the murmur.

ST segment

This is the portion of the QRST complex between the end of the QRS complex and the onset of the T-wave. It corresponds to the onset and early part of ventricular repolarization and represents phase 2 of the transmembrane action potential. Since there is little change in this potential, the ST segment is normally isoelectric. It may be altered by the characteristic patterns of myocardial ischaemia, injury and infarction and by various other cardiac and extracardiac factors. Elevation of the ST segment is seen in acute myocardial infarction, pericarditis and Prinzmetal's angina. It may also occur in acute cor pulmonale, left bundle branch block and left ventricular hypertrophy. Elevation in the anterior chest leads may also be a normal racial variant. Depression of the ST segment is classically seen as a consequence of myocardial ischaemia occurring on exertion. Most commonly there is displacement at the QRS-ST junction (the J point) and characteristically a depression of the first 80 ms of the ST segment. Depression of greater than 2 mm is usually regarded as positive. Non-diagnostic ST and T wave changes are, however, extremely common. These are produced by a wide variety of extracardiac causes and are also relatively common in the normal population.

Standstill

This occurs during failure of impulse generation so that cardiac action is arrested in the resting diastolic state.

Starling curve
see *Frank-Starling mechanism*

Starling effect
see *Frank-Starling mechanism*

Starr-Edwards valve
(A Starr, U.S. surgeon born 1926: M
L Edward, U.S. physician, twentieth
century)
This valvar prosthesis is a caged ball
which has been in increasing use
since its introduction in 1965. It has an
excellent record for durability but, like
all non-biological prostheses, carries
the complication of requiring formal
anticoagulation.

Stenosis
Stenosis is a general word used in
cardiology to denote a narrowing which
obstructs the normal flow of blood. The
term can be applied to heart valves as,
for example, in aortic or mitral stenosis,
or to blood vessels, as in coronary
arterial or carotid arterial stenosis.

Stewart-Hamilton principle
see *Hamilton Stewart principle:
Indicator dilution curve*

Stiff heart syndrome
see *Cardiomyopathy*

Stiffness
Stiffness is a term used to describe the
ratio of a change in pressure to a change
in volume (dP/dV), it is, therefore, the
reciprocal of compliance. In the study
of cardiac dynamics, measurement of
stiffness, in units of mmHg/ml, may be
used to quantitate the properties of the
ventricles and of the walls of the great
arteries.

Stokes-Adams attacks
see *Adams-Stokes disease (syndrome)*

Stokes-Adams syndrome
see *Adams-Stokes disease (syndrome)*

Stone heart
This term describes the appearance and
feel of the heart when it is in a state
of fixed contraction due to massive
overload of calcium in the mitochondria
of myocardial cells. It is a consequence
of global myocardial ischaemia and, most
frequently, occurs following prolonged
cardiopulmonary bypass. The heart of
the surgeon himself must sink when
confronted by such a stone heart,
because recovery from this condition is
improbable.

Storage diseases
There are a large group of systemic
metabolic diseases which, as part of
their overall picture, affect the heart.
The largest group is the storage diseases
where, due to enzymic deficiencies,
substances fail to be degraded and,
instead, build up in the tissues of the
body, including the heart. The diseases
can be categorized in terms of glycogen
storage diseases, ethanolaminoses,
the mucopolysaccharidoses, the
mucolipidoses, disorders of glycoprotein
degradation, acid lipase deficiency, the
sphingolipidoses, and the gangliosidoses.
The more important of these are
discussed at the appropriate point of the
dictionary.

Straddling valves
An atrioventricular valve is said to
straddle when its tension apparatus is
attached within two ventricles, crossing
the plane of a ventricular septal defect
to achieve an attachment within its
morphologically inappropriate ventricle.
Almost always, straddling of the tension
apparatus is accompanied by overriding
of the valvar orifice. See also *Overriding
valves*

Straight back syndrome
This condition is characterized by lack
of normal thoracic kyphosis. It is often
associated with expiratory splitting of
the second heart sound, a parasternal

mid systolic murmur and enlargement of the pulmonary trunk seen on x-ray. For these reasons, it may, on occasions, be confused with an atrial septal defect.

Strain
Strain is defined as the fractional change in any dimension of a material that occurs when a stress is applied to it. For instance, if a material has an unstressed length L and a stressed length L1 then strain can be defined either as L1-L/L (so-called Lagrangian strain) or as the natural logarithm of L1/L (so-called natural strain).

Streptokinase
Streptokinase is a bacterial product that activates the fibrinolytic system. It does this by forming a complex with plasminogen which then activates more plasminogen molecules, resulting ultimately in a state of severe hypofibrinogenaemia. Streptokinase is an effective thrombolytic agent and, currently, is used widely in a number of clinical situations. The most important of these is in the context of acute myocardial infarction due to intracoronary arterial thrombosis where intracoronary or intravenous infusion of streptokinase has been shown to recanalize the occluded vessel in approximately 70% of cases. Such recanalization reperfuses the myocardium and leads to a reduction in the extent of infarction and, therefore, reduced mortality. Streptokinase may also be effective when administered in the context of acute massive pulmonary embolism, acute arterial thrombosis and thrombosis of prosthetic heart valves. Haemorrhagic complications are the main problem associated with its use. The drug is also antigenic and may cause hypotension and anaphylaxis when first administered. Antibodies to streptokinase develop within one week of exposure and prevent its reuse for a period of approximately six months.

Stress
Stress when used in its physical meaning is a measure of the intensity of an applied force. The SI unit of force is the Newton; it is measured in terms of units of force per unit of cross-sectional area. When used in a psychological context, however, stress refers to the pressure imposed by the trials and tribulations of the late twentieth century lifestyle. See also *Personality and coronary arterial disease*

Stress-strain relation
There is a curvilinear relation during passive filling of the ventricles between ventricular stress and ventricular strain. The ratio of stress to strain at any point on this curve is termed the elastic (or chamber) stiffness.

Stress test
see *Exercise electrocardiography*

Stroke volume
Stroke volume is defined as the amount of blood ejected by the left or right ventricle during a single cardiac cycle. It is measured in millilitres.

Strophanthin
see *Digitalis glycosides*

Subaortic conus
see *Subaortic infundibulum*

Subaortic infundibulum
A subaortic infundibulum exists when the leaflets of the aortic valve are supported throughout their circumference by musculature of the ventricular outflow tract. This is a rare finding when the aorta arises, as is usually the case, from the left ventricle. It is the rule, however, when the aorta is connected to the morphologically right ventricle.

Subaortic stenosis
Stenosis of the aortic outflow tract can occur at valvar, supravalvar,

or subvalvar levels. When found at subvalvar level, then the arrangement can vary anatomically according to the morphology of the ventricle which supports the aorta. When, as is usually the case, the aorta arises from the left ventricle, the stenosis can be fixed or dynamic. *Dynamic obstruction* is due to bulging of the ventricular septum, but septal obstruction can also be fixed in the presence of hypertrophic cardiomyopathy. *Fixed obstruction* can be due to a fibrous shelf, to a fibromuscular tunnel, to anomalous attachments of the tension apparatus of atrioventricular valves, or to tissue tags derived from adjacent fibrous structures. All these lesions can also produce obstruction when there is an associated ventricular septal defect, but the commonest anomaly in the latter setting is posterior deviation of the outlet septum. When the aorta arises from the right ventricle, the anatomic substrates producing subaortic obstruction are as seen for the pulmonary trunk when it arises from the right ventricle. See also *Subpulmonary stenosis*

Subpulmonary stenosis
As with the aorta, pulmonary stenosis can be produced at valvar, supravalvar or subvalvar levels. The morphology of the substrates for stenosis reflects the anatomy of the ventricle supporting the trunk. When, as is usually the case, the pulmonary trunk arises from the right ventricle, subpulmonary obstruction is almost always muscular because of the complete muscular infundibulum of the right ventricle. Rarely, it may be due to tissue tags or the spinnaker syndrome. When the pulmonary trunk arises from the left ventricle, the anatomic substrates are the same as for subaortic stenosis.

Subvalvar stenosis
Obstruction of the ventricular outflow tracts is conventionally described as existing at valvar, subvalvar and supravalvar levels. Subvalvar stenosis differs in its morphology depending on whether the morphologically right or left ventricle is involved, these differences reflecting the morphology of the ventricular outflow tracts. Subvalvar obstruction in the right ventricle is almost always muscular, only very rarely being due to causes such as the spinnaker syndrome or gross aneurysm of the membranous septum. Obstruction of the subvalvar area of the left ventricle, in contrast, has a much wider range of causes. Most usually, a fibrous shelf or tunnel obstructs the outlet or there is bulging of the ventricular septum. Alternatively, there may be posterior deviation of the outlet septum co-existing with a ventricular septal defect, an anomalous attachment of the tension apparatus of the left atrioventricular valve, or herniation of fibrous tissue tags from adjacent valvar or septal structures. When co-existing with a ventricular septal defect, subvalvar stenosis may be proximal or distal to the septal deficiency.

Sudden death
Sudden death is death occurring without any pre-existing symptoms of disease. It may be due to cardiological or neurological causes. Cardiological causes include massive anterior infarction and malignant ventricular arrhythmias. It may also occur in association with disorders of the aorta, such as dissection. Neurological disorders are normally catastrophic events such as subarachnoid haemorrhage.

Sudden infant death syndrome
see *Cot death*

Sulcus
This Latin word is used to describe grooves within the heart, such as the atrioventricular, interventricular, interatrial or terminal grooves.

Sulphinpyrazone
This is an antiplatelet drug which interferes with normal synthesis by platelets of thromboxane and prostaglandins, probably by transient inhibition of the enzyme cyclo-oxygenase. Administration of sulphinpyrazone prolongs survival of platelets and may reduce their adhesiveness. When given concurrently with warfarin, sulphinpyrazone reduces the incidence of thromboembolic events in subjects with prosthetic heart valves.

Superior caval syndrome
see *Superior caval venous obstruction*

Superior caval vein
In the normal individual, the superior caval vein is the right-sided venous channel formed by the union of the right and left brachiocephalic veins which then conduct the venous return from the upper body to the right atrium. In some individuals, there can be a left-sided superior caval vein running from the left brachiocephalic vein and terminating in the coronary sinus. This is of functional significance only when the party wall between sinus and left atrium is deficient, because then there can be a right-to-left shunt. Bilateral superior caval veins are also frequently found as part of the complex cardiac malformations seen with isomerism of the atrial appendages.

Superior caval venous obstruction
Obstruction of the superior caval vein is most usually due to malignant disease, although rarely it may be due to external compression of the vein by a hugely dilated aorta. It is also a well recognized late complication of the Mustard operation for complete transposition. Affected subjects have distended non-pulsatile neck veins with oedema of the face and hands and, in severe cases, proptosis. If the diagnosis is in doubt, then angiography or the demonstration of a pressure gradient between the superior caval vein and the right atrium may be helpful. Treatment is either surgical or by balloon dilatation.

Superior limbus
This structure is the upper margin of the oval fossa (fossa ovalis) of the atrial septum. Although often called the 'septum secundum', it is, in reality, produced by an infolding of the interatrial walls.

Superior vena cava
see *Superior caval vein*

Superior vena cava syndrome
see *Superior caval venous obstruction*

Supravalvar stenosis
Stenosis above the level of the aortic valve is due, most frequently, to a pinching in of the aortic wall at the level of the valvar commissures. It is questionable, therefore, whether this form of stenosis is truly supravalvar rather than valvar. This variant is also known as hourglass stenosis. Rarer variants of true supravalvar stenosis are the tubular form, often associated with hypercalcaemia, and the membranous pattern. All forms require surgical treatment. Supravalvar stenosis can also, but more rarely, affect the pulmonary trunk or even a common arterial trunk.

Supraventricular arrhythmias
This collective name is given to rhythm disturbances which arise above the level of the penetrating atrioventricular bundle. It includes arrhythmias at the level of the sinus node, those arising from the atrial myocardium or those produced within the atrial components of the specialized atrioventricular junction.

Supraventricular crest
This muscular structure, also known as the *crista supraventricularis*, is the roof of the morphologically right ventricle between the attachments of the leaflets

of the tricuspid and pulmonary valves. It fuses with the ventricular septum between the limbs of the septomarginal trabeculation (Figure 189).

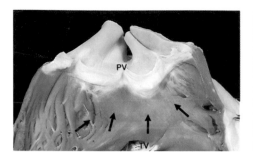

Figure 189. Supraventricular crest. This view of the right ventricle shows the muscular crest (arrowed) separating the leaflets of the tricuspid (TV) and pulmonary (PV) valves.

Supraventricular rhythms
Any rhythm, normal or abnormal, which arises above the non-branching component of the atrioventricular conduction axis is said to be supraventricular.

Supraventricular tachyarrhythmias
This term, now redundant, was applied to any abnormally rapid supraventricular rhythm.

Supraventricular tachycardia
This term describes any supraventricular rhythm which is fast (more than 120 beats per minute). Such rhythms are regular (Figure 190) and can be either paroxysmal, non-paroxysmal or incessant. The paroxysmal forms comprise predominantly the re-entrant tachycardias which involve part or whole of the atrioventricular junction. They are typified by the atrioventricular re-entrant tachycardia associated with the Wolff-Parkinson-White syndrome. Non-paroxysmal supraventricular tachycardia is classically seen in digoxin toxicity. An incessant form of supraventricular

tachycardia usually shows a long R-P interval and may be due to presence of a slowly-conducting accessory atrioventricular pathway.

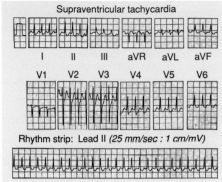

Figure 190. Supraventricular tachycardia. This 12 lead electrocardiogram, along with a rhythm strip, show supraventricular tachycardia with a rapid regular ventricular rate at 220 beats per minute and narrow QRS complexes.

Swan-Ganz catheter
(Harold J C Swan, U.S. cardiologist, born 1922; William Ganz, U.S. cardiologist, born 1919)
see *Balloon catheter*

Swinging heart
This type of excessive cardiac motion is observed in association with large pericardial effusions.

Sydenham's chorea
(Thomas Sydenham, English physician, 1624-1689)
see *Chorea*

Sympathomimetics
see *Inotropic agent*

Syncope
Syncope refers to loss of consciousness due to the impairment (usually temporary) of cerebral perfusion. The

metabolism of the brain, in contrast to that of many other organs, is exquisitely sensitive to perfusion. Consequently, a cessation of flow of cerebral blood leads to loss of consciousness within approximately 10 seconds. A typical syncopal episode is characterized by hypotension, pallor and loss of consciousness in a motionless patient with depressed shallow respirations. When considered in a cardiological context, syncope is most commonly due to the phenomenon of postural hypotension, but it may also result from conduction disturbances or other arrhythmias which cause a profound and sudden reduction in cardiac output. See also *Adams-Stokes disease (syndrome): Aortic stenosis*

Syndrome X

Patients with syndrome X are almost invariably women who present with symptoms typical of angina pectoris with positive exercise tests but who are found at cardiac catheterization to have angiographically normal coronary vessels. The aetiology of the condition is unknown. Coronary arterial spasm is suspected to play a role in some cases, since treatment with antispasmodic calcium blocking drugs such as nifedipine may be helpful. An unspecified proportion of patients with syndrome X subsequently develop a congestive cardiomyopathy. It has been speculated that, in these subjects, angina and electrocardiographic myocardial ischaemia on stress testing is due to a disease process affecting the coronary microcirculation and, therefore, not detectable by conventional coronary angiography.

Syphilitic vascular disease

Syphilis is a venereally transmitted disease caused by chronic infection with a spirochaete organism, *Treponema pallidum*. If the disease is left untreated, 10% of affected subjects ultimately develop cardiovascular manifestations. The commonest of these is aortitis. Direct invasion of the aortic wall by the spirochaete results in an inflammatory process, leading to destruction of the elastic and muscular elements, and their replacement by fibrous tissue which often calcifies and may be visible on a chest x-ray. The ascending aorta is most frequently affected because it has the most generous lymphatic supply. The weakened aortic walls may aneurysmally dilate compressing or eroding adjacent structures. This may then present as bone pain or recurrent laryngeal nerve palsy. Involvement of the aortic sinuses in the disease process may lead to aortic regurgitation. If left untreated, the aorta may rupture. Fibrosis around the origin of the coronary arteries may lead to coronary ostial stenoses and the symptom of angina. Rarely, the spirochaete may invade the myocardium, producing syphilitic gummas. Normally these do not produce symptoms, but occasionally, if the penetrating atrioventricular bundle is affected, heart block may develop.

Systemic arteriovenous fistula

Fistulas between the systemic arteries and veins are communications without any intervening capillary bed. Since veins have a low resistance to flow, this produces the potential for shunting of large quantities of blood in both systole and diastole, resulting in a continuous murmur over the fistula. They produce a high cardiac output, have local manifestations and, when presenting in the neonatal period, may also result in cyanosis because of associated persistent fetal circulation. They are found most commonly as isolated lesions in the head, liver or limbs. They may also be multiple, particularly when found in the skin and mucous membranes as the Osler-Weber-Rendu disease, or hereditary multiple telangiectasia. The best known single fistula is the so-called aneurysm of the vein of Galen. Treatment is by blockage of the feeding artery, either at surgery or by catheter occlusion. See also *Osler-Weber-Rendu disease*

Systemic lupus erythematosus

Subjects afflicted with this severe multisystem disease have developed autoantibodies to components of cell nuclei. Antigen-antibody immune complexes tend to be trapped in vascular and glomerular basement membranes producing local damage through complement activation. Clinical evidence for cardiac involvement is found in approximately half the patients with systemic lupus erythematosus. Pericarditis is the most frequently found cardiac manifestation. Pericardial effusion may be present and the patient may even devleop tamponade. Rarely, pericardial constriction occurs as a late sequel. Vasculitis involving the small myocardial blood vessels may lead to cardiac enlargement and heart failure. Arrhythmias or complete heart block are due to involvement of the penetrating atrioventricular bundle. Endocarditis may also occur and Libman-Sacks vegetations are the characteristic pathological finding. Only rarely is valvar involvement so severe as to cause haemodynamic problems. A small proportion of patients with systemic lupus erythematosus develop pulmonary vascular disease leading to pulmonary hypertension and right heart failure. Most of these patients are also positive for the lupus anticoagulant or anticardiolipin antibody.

Systemic-pulmonary shunts

see *Shunt*

Systemic-to-pulmonary arterial anastomosis

In the strictest sense, any structure connecting the systemic and pulmonary circulations can be described in this fashion. The term is usually reserved, however, for description of shunts created surgically for the palliation of cyanotic congenital heart diseases. The Blalock-Taussig shunt, which uses the patient's own subclavian artery, is the exemplar of these anastomoses. Nowadays, the shunts are usually made from prosthetic material.

Systemic vascular resistance

This represents the resistance between the systemic arteries and the capillary bed, the latter having an assumed pressure of zero. The systemic vascular resistance is given by the ratio of the mean arterial pressure in mmHg divided by systemic blood flow in litres/minute. The normal value is less than 20 resistance units.

Systole

see *Cardiac cycle*

Systolic click murmur syndrome

see *Prolapsing mitral valve syndrome*

Systolic time intervals

The measurement of systolic time intervals is a method of assessing left ventricular function in terms of the timing of well defined events in the cardiac cycle. It is entirely non-invasive and, therefore, normal subjects can be studied in addition to patients. It also has the advantage that repeated measurements can be made in the basal state or after interventions. It is these features that make the measurement of systolic time intervals particularly attractive for the study of drugs with actions on the cardiovascular system. Three systolic time intervals are conventionally measured. The left ventricular ejection time is the time interval over which blood is ejected into the aorta. Electro-mechanical systole is the time from the onset of electrical activation of the left ventricle to the start of relaxation. The pre-ejection period is the interval between the onset of electrical and mechanical activity.

T

T wave
see *Electrocardiogram*

Takayasu's arteritis
(U. Takayasu, Japanese ophthalmologist, born 1871)
This type of arteritis was first noted in 1908, and described a young woman with cataracts and unusual wreath-like arteriovenous anastomoses surrounding the optic papillae. In discussing this case, Takayasu called attention to two patients with similar ocular findings who also had absence of the radial pulses. Subsequently, the disease has been described by a variety of terms reflecting its clinical features, such as aortic arch syndrome, pulseless disease and occlusive thrombo-aortopathy. The condition is reported mainly in Asia and Africa, with a heavy predilection for women. The condition has been subdivided into three types. The first involves primarily the aortic arch and its branches. The second variant spares the aortic arch, but involves the thoraco-abdominal aorta and its branches. The third pattern combines features of both other variants. A specific aetiology has not yet been found. More than half the patients initially develop a systemic illness followed by a latent period of variable duration. After the latent period, signs develop referable to the obliterative changes in the vessels. Late manifestations therefore include diminished or absent pulses, hypertension and heart failure. Steroids are effective in relieving constitutional symptoms in the acute systemic phase of the disease. Indeed, there is some evidence that continued administration of steroids may retard progression of arterial narrowing during the later stages of the disease. Anticoagulants are recommended for treatment and prevention of transient ischaemic symptoms. In severe cases, surgical treatment may be necessary, including endarterectomy, bypass of obstructed arteries and/or resection of localized aneurysms. The course of the disease is unpredictable but slow progression over a few years is the usual outcome.

Tamponade
Tamponade exists when fluid collects within the pericardial cavity in sufficient quantities to compromise the action of the heart. This can be a chronic event, as with gradual collection of an effusion, or an acute event due to trauma or rupture of the myocardial wall as the consequence of infarction. It is essential to decompress the pericardium, or the situation rapidly becomes fatal.

Taussig-Bing anomaly
(Helen Brooke Taussig, U.S. physician, 1898-1898; Richard J. Bing, U.S. surgeon, born 1909)
The heart initially described by Taussig and Bing in 1954 has become the source of some controversy. The congenital malformation is certainly characterized by aortic origin from the right ventricle, and by the orifice of the pulmonary trunk overriding a ventricular septal defect. The argument concerns the precise ventriculoarterial connexion, which is intermediate between a discordant connexion and double outlet from the right ventricle, and whether cases should, like the original, have a bilaterally complete infundibulum to qualify for eponymous description. A pragmatic approach is to define the Taussig-Bing anomaly in terms of the overriding of the septum by the pulmonary trunk in the presence of right ventricular origin of the aorta (Figure 191), and then to accept that the ventriculoarterial connexion can vary between double outlet and discordant. It seems churlish to exclude cases simply because they have fibrous continuity between the leaflets of the mitral and pulmonary valves.

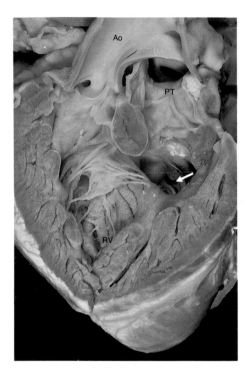

Figure 191. Taussig-Bing anomaly. This illustration shows a typical example of the lesion known as the Taussig-Bing anomaly. The pulmonary trunk (PT) arises mostly from the right ventricle (RV) and overrides a sub-pulmonary ventricular septal defect (arrowed). The aorta (Ao) also arises from the right ventricle.

Tawara's node
(Sunao Tawara, Japanese pathologist, 1873-1938)
see *Atrioventricular node*

Tay-Sachs disease
(Warren Tay, English physician, 1843-1927: Bernard Parney Sachs, U.S. neurologist, 1858-1944)
see *Gangliosidoses*

Technetium-99m
This is the commonest radionuclide used in nuclear medicine, its popularity reflecting the fact that it can be incorporated into a wide variety of molecules. It has a half-life of six hours and it is produced from a bench top generator by elution from the mother radionuclide (molybdenum-99) on an ion exchange resin. Labelling of erythrocytes allows imaging of the intracardiac blood pools, and is usually performed with sequential intravenous injections of 5 mg stannous pyrophosphate and 740 MBq of sodium pertechnetate. The mechanism of labelling is not fully understood but, within a number of seconds of injection, the stannous ion reduces the pertechnetate to a more chemically active form which binds to proteins within the red cells. In the absence of stannous ion, free pertechnetate is taken up by the thyroid gland, stomach, kidney, and bone. See also *Radionuclide ventriculography*

Temporal arteritis
see *Giant cell arteritis*

Tendinous cords
(*also known as* Chordae tendineae)
The atrioventricular valves, unlike the arterial valves, have an extensive tension apparatus which prevents their excursion into the atria during ventricular systole. The part of the apparatus between the edges of the leaflets and the papillary muscles is made up of the tendinous cords. These differ in their structure, and can be described in terms of first and second order cords, depending on the pattern of branching, or basal cords which connect the undersurface of the leaflets directly to the ventricular myocardium. So-called commissural, cleft and strut cords are particular patterns of first order cords, supporting either gaps between the leaflets or strengthening their ventricular surfaces.

Tendon of Todaro
(Francesco Todaro, Italian anatomist, born 1839)

This tendinous structure, also known as the *sinus streiffen*, is a fibrous cord which extends into the sinus septum from the commissure of the Eustachian and Thebesian valves, running forward to insert into the central fibrous body. Its importance is that it forms the atrial border of the triangle of Koch, thus forming a vital surgical landmark to the location of the atrial components of the atrioventricular conduction axis.

Terminal crest
(*also known as* Crista terminalis)
This prominent ridge of muscle forms the boundary between the venous component of the right atrium and the atrial appendage. The pectinate muscles of the appendage arise in serried ranks at right angles to the crest.

Terminal groove
This groove marks the external location of the terminal crest, separating the venous component of the right atrium from its appendage. Its clinical importance comes from the fact that the sinus node lies immediately subepicardially within the groove, usually lateral to the crest of the appendage. See also *Sinus node*

Tetrad, Fallot's
see *Fallot's tetralogy*

Tetralogy of Fallot
see *Fallot's tetralogy*

Thalidomide and cardiovascular malformations
The tragedy of congenital malformations resulting from administration of the drug thalidomide during the first trimester of pregnancy is now part of the history of the science of teratology. Usually recognized with regard to the shortened limbs which resembled flippers of seals (phocomelia), ingestion of thalidomide also produced malformations within the heart, notably tetralogy of Fallot, septal

defects, and common arterial trunk. These should, however, now be a thing of the past in this context.

Thallium-201
Thallium-201 is a radionuclide produced by a cyclotron with a physical half-life of 72 hours. Clearance from the bloodstream is rapid following intravenous injection, with approximately 95% clearance after the first circulation, although only 5% of the injected dose is taken up by the myocardium. Myocardial distribution is proportional to myocardial blood flow over a wide range of values, hence its efficacy. See also *Myocardial perfusion imaging*

Thebesian valve
(Adam Christian Thebesius, German physician, 1686-1732)
During development, there are extensive folds of tissue which function as valves between the venous and atrial components of the heart. With completion of formation of the heart chamber, the primitive venous component is incorporated within the right atrium, and the folds persist as fibrous valves related to the mouths of the inferior caval vein and the coronary sinus. The valve of the coronary sinus is known as the Thebesian valve. Rarely, it can be imperforate and block the venous return from the myocardium entering the right atrium.

Thermodilution
see *Indicator dilution curves*

Thiazide diuretics
Drugs of basic benzene disulphonamide composition which have diuretic properties.

Third heart sound
An S3 gallop (or third heart sound) is the name given to a low pitched noise which occurs in early diastole and which can be appreciated by auscultation. Exactly

how the third heart sound is produced is unknown but Doppler, echocardiographic and phonocardiographic studies clearly show that its timing is associated with the peak velocity of ventricular filling and the termination of the rapid rate of change of ventricular volume during early diastole.

A third heart sound may be physiological or pathological. Physiological sounds occur normally in young subjects (less than 30 years old), when their presence seems to be associated with high cardiac output and sympathetic drive. A physiological third heart sound may also be found in older subjects with normal hearts but who have anaemia or thyrotoxicosis.

A pathological third heart sound may be heard in conditions where the ventricle is volume loaded, such as mitral regurgitation, or when the myocardium is diseased (for instance, cardiomyopathy). They are also heard in constrictive pericarditis, where classically the timing of the third heart sound is early *(the pericardial knock)*.

Third heart sounds can arise from either the right or left ventricles. A right ventricular third heart sound can be distinguished by its distribution (loudest at the left sternal edge) and by the fact that it is intensified by inspiration and is associated with a rapid Y descent in the jugular venous pressure.

Thoracic outlet syndrome

Pain in the arm and paraesthesia in the ulnar nerve distribution is characteristic of the thoracic outlet syndrome. It is caused by compression of the brachial plexus by a cervical rib or by a tight scalene anterior muscle. Its importance to cardiologists is that it produces symptoms which on superficial inquiry may be confused with those of angina pectoris.

Thorel's bundle

(Charles Thorel, German anatomist, 1868-1935)

In 1909, Thorel claimed to have demonstrated a bundle of specialized conduction tissue which ran along the terminal crest to join the sinus and atrioventricular nodes. Few were convinced by his findings which have not subsequently been confirmed.

Thrill

In the cardiological vocabulary, a thrill is simply a palpable cardiac murmur.

Thromboembolic pulmonary hypertension

This is pulmonary hypertension resulting from recurrent pulmonary thromboembolism. The disease is normally far advanced when it first presents usually with symptoms of dyspnoea, fatigue, chest pain and haemoptysis. The clinical findings are those of an elevated venous pressure with a dominant A wave, a right ventricular heave and palpable pulmonary closure sound and on auscultation a gallop rhythm and loud pulmonary closure of the second heart sound. The electrocardiogram normally shows features of right ventricular hypertrophy and strain, and the chest x-ray classically shows large proximal pulmonary arteries with pruning of the distal vessels and oligaemic peripheral lung fields. Frequently a search for the source of emboli is fruitless although on occasions thrombus may be found in the veins of the legs, pelvis and arms and in the right atrial appendage. The diagnosis is made on clinical grounds and on the appearances of the pulmonary angiogram which classically shows non-uniform obstruction of the major branches of the pulmonary artery. However, in the advanced stages of the disease the pulmonary angiographic appearances are indistinguishable from those found in primary pulmonary hypertension.

A substantial number of patients with thromboembolic pulmonary hypertension have altered platelet function and blood hypercoagulability as a prominent feature and this is often related to some form of autoimmune disease.

The treatment of thromboembolic pulmonary hypertension is most unsatisfactory. Long-term anticoagulation with warfarin seldom halts the disease process. Likewise, plication of the inferior vena cava or the insertion of a caval umbrella to prevent further embolism seems to be unhelpful as alternative channels for venous blood to return to the right heart soon develop. Heart-lung transplantation is a therapeutic option but thromboembolic disease may then begin to affect the transplanted lungs.

Thromboendarterectomy, coronary

This surgical term describes an incision within a coronary artery for the purpose of removing thrombus and its associated atherosclerotic plaque as a prelude to coronary arterial bypass grafting. Although controversial, most evidence would seem to indicate that patency of grafts is inferior when they are attached to endarterectomized vessels. The usual practice, therefore, is to graft to more distal arteries, while thrombosis would now be treated by thrombolysis in the early stages.

Thrombolysis

Thrombolysis is the breaking down and dissolution of blood clots. Intravascular thrombus is naturally broken down by the body's fibrinolytic system but this process can be hastened and enhanced by thrombolytic agents such as streptokinase, urokinase and tissue plasminogen activator. The concept of thrombolysis has now assumed a central key role in cardiology because several large multicentre studies have shown that thrombolytic therapy given to patients in the acute phase of myocardial infarction

is effective in recanalizing occluded coronary vessels in approximately 70% of cases, resulting in less myocardial damage and therefore reduced early and late mortality from infarction. All the studies show that thrombolytic therapy is most effective when given within four hours of the onset of chest pain and that subjects with anterior infarcts tend to benefit more than subjects with inferior infarcts. The best thrombolytic agent is not yet known but clinical trials are currently in progress to answer this question.

Thrombosis

The process of thrombosis is the formation of clots within the circulatory system. In cardiology, the significance of thrombosis is greatest with regard to myocardial infarction. Although the role of thrombosis had been controversial, there is now overwhelming evidence that infarction is the result of thrombosis occurring on the surface of damaged atherosclerotic plaques. Thrombotic events are also seen elsewhere, as in mural thrombus formed in the aftermath of infarction. Thrombotic material can also be detached and carried within the blood stream, a process known as thromboembolism.

Thrombotic endocarditis

This disease process of the cardiac valves, affecting their endocardial surfaces in the absence of bacterial infection, can accompany a variety of diseases. It is also known as non-bacterial thrombotic, or marantic, endocarditis. Multiple verrucous vegetations are formed which adhere to the lines of closure of the valvar leaflets, particularly in the mitral (Figure 192) and aortic valves. The distinction from infective endocarditis is made histologically because of the absence of involvement of the leaflets themselves in the process of disease, the lesions being confined to the valvar surfaces.

Thrombotic endocarditis

The process is seen mostly in patients with malignant disease and, usually, is an incidental autopsy finding. It can, however, present clinically as a consequence of thromboembolism to the cerebral or coronary arteries, sometimes producing myocardial infarction.

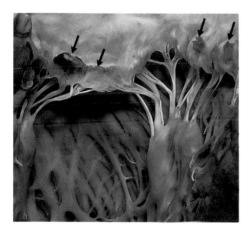

Figure 192. Thrombotic endocarditis. This illustration shows the lesions of thrombotic endocarditis (arrowed) on the leaflets of the mitral valve. *(Reproduced with the kind permission of Professor A.E.Becker)*

Thromboxane A

Thromboxane A is a substance formed in platelets which plays a central role in the formation of a thrombus following vascular injury. Thromboxane A causes platelet release and aggregation and is a potent vasoconstrictor. Thromboxane A_2 is a metabolite of arachidonic acid. Arachidonic acid is oxygenated by the enzyme cyclo-oxygenase to form the intermediate substance prostaglandin G_2. Thromboxane synthetase then converts prostaglandin G_2 to thromboxane A. Aspirin, by inhibiting cyclo-oxygenase, thereby prevents thromboxane A production.

Thrombus

see *Thrombosis*

Thyrotoxic heart disease

The most common cardiac manifestation of thyrotoxicosis is sinus tachycardia, with or without supraventricular arrhythmias. In association with the increase in heart rate thus produced, there is an increased cardiac output, increased coronary blood flow and raised oxygen consumption by the myocardium. The patient with thyrotoxic heart disease may, therefore, show features typical of a high cardiac output syndrome. If untreated and persistent, further cardiac complications may develop, including congestive heart failure and, occasionally, exacerbation of or unmasking of angina pectoris. Treatment is aimed at the basic underlying thyrotoxic condition. It is usual to administer additional beta blockers to control the increased heart rate.

Tietze's syndrome

(Alexander Tietze, German surgeon, 1864-1927)
This syndrome is characterized by pain and swelling of the costochondral or xiphisternal joints. Its aetiology is unknown but, once established, it may persist for many months. Its importance is that the patient may not appreciate the superficiality of the pain and may wrongly ascribe the symptoms to heart disease. The condition is totally benign.

Tilting disc valves

These are mechanical heart valves in which the flow of blood is controlled by a tilting disc which opens and closes passively in response to generated pressure gradients. Examples of tilting disc valves are the Lillihei-Kastor prosthesis, the Ionescu-Shiley prosthesis and, most widely used, the Bjork-Shiley prosthesis. Tilting disc valves are reliable and long lasting but haemodynamically they are mildly obstructive, they may cause haemolysis, and they are subject to thrombosis unless anticoagulation is given after implantation.

Timolol
Timolol is a non-selective beta-adrenergic antagonist agent with no intrinsic sympathomimetic activity. It is effective treatment in the management of chronic stable angina pectoris and systemic hypertension. The results of a Norwegian multicentre study show that the administration of timolol to patients following acute myocardial infarction has a protective effect, lowering mortality at one year by 40%.

Tissue-type plasminogen activator
see *Thrombolysis*

Tocainide
Tocainide is a class 1 antiarrhythmic agent which has a longer half life and a higher oral bioavailability than lignocaine of which it is a structural analogue. Tocainide may be effective in the management of life-threatening ventricular arrhythmias but, unfortunately, its high incidence of serious side-effects, particularly bone marrow suppression, limits its clinical utility.

Tomography
Tomography is a form of imaging which produces slices of an object instead of a projection onto a plane such as is formed in a conventional chest x-ray. The technique can be applied in many fields but is most widely encountered as computed tomography using x-rays (x-ray computed tomography [CT]), or gamma rays (emission computed tomography, either single photon [SPECT] or positrons [PET]). It relies upon acquiring planar images in many different projections around the object, and from these using a computer to reconstruct the image of a slice through the object. See also *Positron emission tomography: Single photon emission computed tomography*

Torsade de pointes
This ventricular tachycardia is characterized by electrocardiographic QRS complexes of changing amplitude which appear to twist around the isoelectric line (Figure 193). The ventricular rate is usually 200–250 beats per minute. It is seen when there is prolonged ventricular repolarization. This may be congenital or acquired, and can be secondary to bradycardia, electrolyte disorders, or antiarrhythmic drugs. While frequently terminating spontaneously, the rhythm disturbance is potentially lethal because of its tendency to degenerate into ventricular fibrillation. Treatment of the congenital form is usually with beta blockade. Acute treatment requires manoeuvres to shorten ventricular repolarization, such as pacing, until the precipitating factor has been removed.

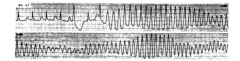

Figure 193. Torsade de pointes. This ambulatory electrocardiographic recording from a patient with QT prolongation shows the onset of torsade de pointes with the characteristic spiralling of the QRS complexes.

Total artificial heart
The so-called 'total' artificial heart is a mechanical device which totally replaces the pumping functions of the native heart. Various machines have been designed and implanted but the concept is, as yet, still in the experimental stage. The main impetus to continued development in this field is the chronic shortage of donor hearts for transplantation.

Totally anomalous pulmonary venous connexion

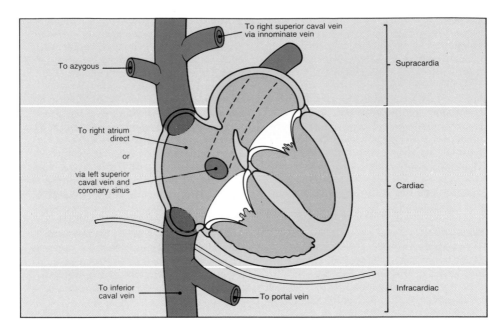

To right superior caval vein
via innominate vein

To azygous

To right atrium
direct

or

via left superior
caval vein and
coronary sinus

To inferior
caval vein

To portal vein

Supracardia

Cardiac

Infracardiac

Figure 194. Totally anomalous venous connexion. This diagram shows the variability possible when all the pulmonary veins are connected to a site other than left atrium.

Totally anomalous pulmonary venous connexion

Connexions of the pulmonary veins are said to be totally anomalous when all the venous drainage from the lungs is to a site other than the morphologically left atrium. Usually, the anomalously connecting veins join together into a confluence before connecting to a systemic venous structure (Figure 194). This may be to a vein within the thorax (supracardiac connexion); to the right atrium, usually via the coronary sinus (cardiac connexion); or to a vein within the abdomen (infracardiac and infradiaphragmatic connexion). More rarely, the pulmonary veins may connect individually to anomalous sites (mixed anomalous connexion). Unless treated surgically, the congenital malformation is fatal. It presents with cyanosis in infancy,

the most severe cases being those with obstructed pathways of drainage. This is seen most frequently with infracardiac connexion, where the drainage is usually to the portal venous system. Then, once the venous duct is closed, all blood must traverse the hepatic sinusoids to reach the heart. Nowadays, all forms of totally anomalous connexion are diagnosed by cross-sectional echocardiography and submitted immediately for surgical correction. Mortality rates are now less than 10% for the overall group in the best centres, and are improving all the time. The malformation is corrected by anastomosing the anomalous veins to the morphologically left atrium and closing the atrial septal defect which is a universal accompaniment of the lesion.

Trabecula, septomarginal, septomarginalis
see *Septomarginal trabecula*

Transaminase
see *Serum cardiac enzymes*

Transcatheter ablation

This is the use of electrical energy (delivered via temporary transvenous pacing catheters) to destroy parts of the conduction system, accessory pathways or arrhythmic focuses. The technique has now become established for the creation of complete heart block by destroying normal atrioventricular conduction in order to control drug-resistant supraventricular arrhythmias. High energy shocks of direct current up to 320 joules are commonly used but radiofrequency alternating current has also been used.

Transluminal coronary angioplasty

see *Angioplasty*

Transmembrane resting potential

This is the potential difference across the membrane of a cardiac cell during electrical diastole.

Transplantation

Transplantation of the heart was first performed in humans in 1967 but, as a result of the high mortality rates resulting from graft rejection, most centres which embarked on this procedure in those early days subsequently abandoned the procedure as a therapeutic option. In the late 1970s and early 1980s, however, as rejection became better understood and better treated, cardiac transplantation was resumed. It is now part of the standard armamentarium of most major institutions for the treatment of left and right ventricular disease.

Currently, transplantation of the heart is reserved for patients with advanced heart disease who are usually in class III or IV of the classification of the New York Heart Association. Eventual recipients should have a poor prognosis for survival for one year. It is clear from many research studies that younger patients have a significantly better rate of survival and so the upper age limit for potential recipients in most centres is between 50 and 55 years. Contraindications to cardiac transplantation (although some of these patients may be amenable to heart-lung transplantation) include severe pulmonary hypertension, parenchymal pulmonary disease, diabetes mellitus requiring insulin, donor-specific cytotoxic antibodies and concomitant metastatic disease. The commonest indications are ischaemic cardiomyopathy and idiopathic cardiomyopathies. Donor hearts are from patients who have sustained irreversible cerebral damage. Sources of donor supply have broadened following the success of transport using hypothermic techniques to prevent ischaemia. The procedure is performed under cardiopulmonary bypass, when the recipient heart is removed, leaving the posterior walls of the atria and their venous connexions in place. The donor atria are then sutured to the corresponding structures inside the residual atria of the recipient and the great arteries anastomosed last. In the absence of rejection, the transplanted heart (which is denervated) has the capacity to maintain normal cardiac output. The current survival rate at major centres following heart transplantation is in the region of 75–80% at one year. Survival figures are improving all the time, largely as a result of the effectiveness of the newly used immunosuppressive agent, cyclosporin. Until a few years ago, *heart-lung transplantation* was rarely practiced. But, over the last few years, there has been a remarkable growth in this field. This is usually performed for conditions associated with severe pulmonary vascular disease, including the Eisenmenger syndrome and primary pulmonary hypertension and, to a lesser extent, for primary disorders of the lung, including cystic fibrosis. Heart-lung transplantation is beset by the same problems as cardiac transplantation, particularly rejection. See also *Rejection*

Transposition

This term is used loosely in the vocabulary of congenital heart disease. Nowadays, when used in isolation, it almost always describes a discordant ventriculoarterial connexion, in other words, the situation in which the aorta is connected to the morphologically right ventricle (or its rudiment) and the pulmonary trunk to the morphologically left ventricle (or its rudiment). In the past, transposition was used to describe any malformed heart in which the aorta was positioned anteriorly to the pulmonary trunk. A few centres still use this convention. For this reason, it is more precise to speak of the discordant connexion, or to qualify 'transposition' with an adjective such as complete or congenitally corrected. See also *Transposition complexes*

Transposition complexes

As presently used, describing only one feature of the heart (the ventriculoarterial junction), hearts with 'transposition' can exist in varied forms and guises. It is the overall group of hearts with a discordant ventriculoarterial connexion which, usually, are described as the transposition complexes. The variability within the group reflects primarily the arrangement at the atrioventricular junction. Thus, with a concordant atrioventricular connexion, the combination produces parallel patterns of circulation known as complete transposition. With a discordant atrioventricular connexion, the two discordances cancel out to give a physiologically normal pattern of circulation, hence the term congenitally corrected transposition. The discordant ventriculoarterial connexion, however, can also be found with double inlet ventricle, with absence of one atrioventricular connexion, or with an ambiguous and biventricular atrioventricular connexion. In all these instances, the influence of the discordant connexion at the ventriculoarterial junction (transposition) is modified by both the atrioventricular connexion and by other associated malformations. These, together with the prevailing haemodynamics, must all be determined if we are to unravel the intricacies of the transposition complexes.

Traube's sign

(Ludwig Traube, German physician and pathologist, 1818-1876)
see *Pistol shot femoral arteries*

Triangle, Einthoven

see *Einthoven triangle*

Triangle of Koch

see *Koch's triangle*

Tricuspid atresia

This important congenital cardiac malformation is characterized by complete blockage of the usual exit from the right atrium to the right ventricle. Although often conceptualized in terms of an imperforate tricuspid valve (Figure 195a), this variety of tricuspid atresia is very rare. Much more frequently (over nine-tenths of cases), the entire atrioventricular connexion is absent, and the right atrium has a muscular floor (Figure 195b). At any event, all the systemic venous return must cross the obliterated atrial septal defect to the left atrium, and the right ventricle, which is usually rudimentary and incomplete, is fed through a ventricular septal defect. Variability exists in the ventriculoarterial connexion, and in the degree of obstruction of pulmonary arterial flow which is often described using an alphanumeric code. It is better to describe these features separately and precisely. Infants with the lesion usually present with cyanosis, most severe in the presence of pulmonary arterial obstruction. Diagnosis is now made most readily by cross-sectional

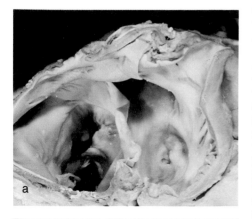

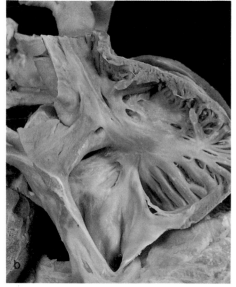

Figure 195. Tricuspid atresia. These two views of the right atrium in patients with tricuspid atresia show the very rare variant produced by an imperforate tricuspid valve (a) and the more common pattern of absence of the atrioventricular connexion (b).

echocardiography, which shows the absent atrioventricular connexion, the cause of the ventricular septal defect, the ventriculoarterial connexion and the nature of the associated anomalies.

Treatment must, eventually, be surgical by means of the Fontan procedure or one of its modifications. Most centres, at present, do not undertake the Fontan operation during infancy, which is when the majority of patients present, so initial treatment is almost always palliative. A systemic to pulmonary arterial shunt is constructed when pulmonary blood flow is restricted, while the pulmonary trunk is banded in the face of excessive pulmonary arterial flow. The Fontan procedure, or a modification, is then usually performed after the second year of life. Results of surgery are improving all the time, and mortality rates of less than 10% are now achieved in the best centres, although the risk is considerably higher in complex cases. The long-term outlook, however, remains uncertain, since the efficacy of the right atrium in supporting the pulmonary circulation over an entire lifetime has yet to be determined.

Tricuspid regurgitation

Regurgitation across the morphologically tricuspid valve is usually functional in origin, being secondary to right ventricular dilatation with expansion of the tricuspid orifice. More rarely, it is the result of organic disease, such as rheumatic involvement of the leaflets, interruption of valve function by a right atrial tumour, or presence of congenital anomalies, particularly Ebstein's malformation. Symptomatology is dominated by the underlying lesion. The physical signs are of elevated venous pressure with a pansystolic murmur best heard at the base of the heart. In severe cases, there may be an associated right ventricular third heart sound. The liver is characteristically pulsatile and enlarged. Management should be aimed at the underlying problem but, in rare cases, surgery becomes necessary. This often takes the form of annuloplasty although replacement of the valve may sometimes be necessary.

Tricuspid stenosis
This is very rarely a lone lesion, usually being accompanied by mitral stenosis. The most common aetiology is rheumatic, but it may also occur in association with carcinoid tumours, Ebstein's malformation, and, rarely, a right atrial tumour or the spinnaker syndrome may produce a clinical picture which resembles tricuspid stenosis. Symptomatology is normally dominated by associated lesions, but peripheral oedema may be present, often with hepatomegaly. Physical signs are those of a dominant 'a' wave, noted in the venous pressure trace, together with a right-sided opening snap and a mid-diastolic murmur. Management is usually by means of diuretics to relieve peripheral oedema. If surgery becomes necessary, either valvotomy or valvar replacement are the appropriate operations.

Tricuspid valve
The tricuspid valve is the atrioventricular valve of the morphologically right ventricle. Its three leaflets are located septally, antero-superiorly and inferior or murally (Figure 196). The most characteristic feature, in comparison with the mitral valve, is the presence of tendinous cords tethering the septal leaflet to the inlet component of the ventricular septum. It is a rule that valves 'go' with ventricles so, in the usual variant of hearts with a discordant atrioventricular connexion, the tricuspid valve is a left rather than right-sided structure, guarding the junction between the left atrium and the morphologically right ventricle.

Tricuspid valve prolapse
This is the mechanism of prolapse of the leaflets of the tricuspid valve similar to that afflicting the mitral valve. It is most commonly due to so-called floppy degeneration of the leaflets. It can produce an ejection click. See also *Prolapsed mitral valve syndrome*

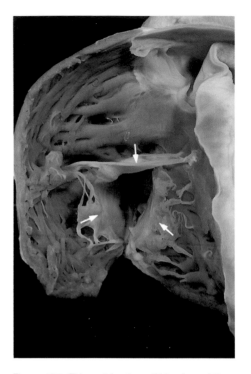

Figure 196. Tricuspid valves. This view of the right ventricle shows the three leaflets of the tricuspid valve (arrowed).

Triggered automaticity
This mechanism of arrhythmogenesis is characterized by pacemaker activity which occurs as a consequence of generation of an abnormal impulse or series of impulses. In the absence of these impulses, generated within the cells themselves rather than within a recognized component of the conduction system, the cells would remain quiescent. The triggered activity is initiated by afterpotentials, these being depolarizations of the cell of low amplitude which occur during early or late repolarization. Although demonstrated in experimental preparations, no certain evidence for this mechanism exists as yet in man.

Triglycerides
see *Lipid*

Trigona fibrosa cordis
see *Fibrous trigones*

Truncal valves
The truncal valve is the common valve guarding the orifice of a common aterial trunk. See also *Common arterial trunk*

Truncus
see *Common arterial trunk*

Trypanosoma cruzi
This is the protozoan organism which is the cause of Chagas' disease.

Tumours
Tumours can affect the heart (although this is not a common phenomenon) and they may be primary or secondary. See also *Angioma: Angiosarcoma: Cardiac tumours: Haemangiosarcoma: Lipoma: Myxoma: Rhabdomyoma: Rhabdomyosarcoma*

Tunnel, aortico-left ventricular
This rare congenital cardiac malformation takes the form of a tubular communication between the outflow tract of the left ventricle and one of the aortic sinuses, thus producing the substrate for aortic regurgitation and presenting with the diastolic murmur of aortic incompetence. Recently, it has been suggested that the lesion is a defect in the wall of the right coronary sinus rather than a tunnel. Almost without exception, it involves the right coronary sinus of Valsalva, producing gross aneurysmal dilatation of the sinus. It usually presents in infancy, and is the most likely diagnosis in any child of less than two years with aortic incompetence. Immediate surgical repair is mandatory in the hope of preventing residual valvar incompetence. Often, this persists despite closure of the defect, and then replacement of the valve is necessary.

Type A behaviour as risk of coronary arterial disease
see *Personality and coronary arterial disease: Stress*

Type B behaviour
see *Personality and coronary arterial disease: Stress*

341

U

U-wave

This is a diastolic potential seen on the surface electrocardiogram at the end of the T-wave. Its genesis is unclear, but is believed to be either a consequence of repolarization of Purkinje fibres or mechanical diastolic relaxation of the myocardium. In amplitude, it may reach half the size of the T-wave and is usually most obvious in leads V2 and V3. Abnormalities of the U-wave may be produced by hypokalaemia or during treatment with amiodarone, when it tends to increase in amplitude. It is also seen in hypertension and left ventricular hypertrophy when it becomes inverted.

Uhl's anomaly

(Henry Stephen Magraw Uhl, U.S. physician, born 1921)
This very rare congenital cardiac anomaly is characterized by complete absence of the parietal musculature of the morphologically right ventricle with normal formation of the tricuspid and pulmonary valves, the septal structures and the left ventricle. The absence of the parietal myocardium produces a parchment ventricular wall. The lesion, however, must be distinguished from the gross thinning and dilatation of the right ventricle found with Ebstein's malformation and pulmonary atresia, and from fatty infiltration of the myocardium seen in right ventricular dysplasia. True Uhl's anomaly is probably best treated by the Fontan procedure, although true cases of this exceedingly rare lesion are mostly reported at autopsy rather than diagnosed during life.

Ultrasound

see *Echocardiography*

Unicuspid unicommissural valve stenosis

This description is given to the type of valvar stenosis characterized by fusion of two of the three commissures of the normal valve. The effect is that of a single leaflet with an eccentric opening at the site of the persisting commissure (Figure 197). The pattern is almost always seen in the aortic valve, the keyhole opening being adjacent to the mitral valve. It is the commonest type of lesion seen with critical aortic stenosis presenting in infancy.

Figure 197. Unicuspid unicommissural valve stenosis. This dissection of a stenosed aortic valve shows a solitary commissure in a domed valve in which raphes represents the site of fusion in an initially three leaflet valve.

Unipolar leads

This describes an electrocardiographic recording lead consisting of an exploring electrode in contact with the body surface or directly with the heart. The recordings from the leads are compared to some reference point, which may be another lead, usually attached to one of the limbs, or an electrical reference point such as a central terminal. The chest leads, for example, are unipolar leads recorded between the six chest positions and the central terminal.

Univentricular atrioventricular connexion

This term has been introduced in recent years as a generic name for the group of congenitally malformed hearts in which the atria are connected to only one ventricle. Previously described in terms of 'univentricular hearts', this terms is less than satisfactory because most hearts deformed in this manner possess two ventricles, albeit that one is dominant and the other is incomplete and rudimentary. The atrioventricular connexions producing a univentricular arrangement are double inlet along with absence of either the right or the left atrioventricular connexion. Each of these three patterns can exist with the atria connected to a dominant left ventricle, the right ventricle being incomplete and rudimentary; to a dominant right ventricle with an incomplete and rudimentary left ventricle; or to a solitary and indeterminate ventricle. Further variability is then possible in terms of the ventriculoarterial connexions and associated malformations. The term 'univentricular atrioventricular connexion', therefore, is not a diagnosis in itself, but rather a means of distinguishing that group of hearts with the atria connected to one ventricle from the much larger group in which each atrium is connected to its own ventricle *(biventricular atrioventricular connexions)*. The commonest examples of hearts with a univentricular connexion are those with tricuspid atresia and those with double inlet left ventricle.

Univentricular heart

In its literal sense, this term is best used to describe congenitally malformed hearts possessing a solitary ventricular chamber. Such hearts, however, are exceedingly rare. In the past, the term has been used illogically to define hearts having a double inlet atrioventricular connexion. This convention was unsatisfactory for two reasons. First, most hearts with double inlet have two ventricles, one being dominant and the other rudimentary and incomplete. Second, the definition of 'univentricular heart' traditionally excluded patients with atrioventricular valvar atresia, despite the fact that ventricular morphology in the majority of these patients resembles that found in those with double inlet ventricle. It is better, therefore, to group these hearts together on the basis of their univentricular atrioventricular connexion, recognizing that only very rarely is the ventricular mass truly univentricular. The term 'univentricular heart', nonetheless, continues to be used as though synonymous with a double inlet atrioventricular connexion.

Unstable angina

(also known as Acute coronary insufficiency: Crescendo angina: Pre-infarction angina) Unstable angina is clinically important because it often heralds subsequent myocardial infarction. The condition is defined as angina which occurs at rest or on minimal exertion in the absence of electrocardiographic or cardiac enzymic changes of infarction. The discomfort experienced by the patient in the chest is similar in quality to that of classic effort-induced angina but is usually both more intense and more prolonged. The diagnosis is normally confirmed on the basis of the history together with minor changes seen on the

Unstable angina

electrocardiogram which often shows
transient deviations of the ST segment
(either depression or elevation) or
isolated changes in the T waves.
In terms of pathophysiology, the
condition usually represents severe
obstructive coronary arterial disease
with acute plaque rupture. Some cases,
however, are the result of coronary
arterial spasm, either superimposed on
obstructive coronary arterial disease or
occurring in isolation *(true Prinzmetal
angina)*.
Since the condition is serious, and
potentially lethal, management must
be aggressive. The patient should be
admitted to hospital and immediately
placed on bed rest. Initial therapy is
usually administration of nitrates given
by the intravenous route. Calcium
antagonists are also usually prescribed,
as are beta blockers, though the latter
should be avoided in cases of true
Prinzmetal angina. Agents to prevent
platelet stickiness are also given (such
as aspirin, persantin, or a combination
of the two) and the patient should be
referred for cardiac catheterization.

Urokinase

Urokinase is a thrombolytic agent
found naturally in human urine but
it is produced commercially from
culture of fetal kidney cells. It acts
on the endogenous fibrinolytic system
by promoting conversion of inactive
plasminogen to the proteolytic enzyme
plasmin which degrades fibrin. Urokinase
has been shown to be as effective
as streptokinase in the treatment of
pulmonary embolism, thrombosed
artificial heart valves and other
major arterial or venous thrombosis.
Remarkably, given the current intense
interest in the field, there are few reports
of its use in the clinical context of acute
myocardial infarction.

V

V leads
see *Electrocardiogram*

V-max
This symbol describes the maximum velocity of shortening of the contractile elements of the ventricles during systole.

V-waves
V-waves are the waves seen in the tracings of the cardiac cycle or in the jugular venous pulse which are related to ventricular contraction. See also *Central venous pressure: Jugular venous pulse*

Valsalva manoeuvre
(Antonio Maria Valsalva, Italian anatomist and physician, 1666–1723)
This manoeuvre is the result of prolonged forced expiration against a closed glottis followed by a sudden release of pressure. Intrathoracic pressure is raised, and then falls suddenly when the strain is released. Continuous recordings of heart rate and systemic arterial pressure reveal that the Valsalva manoeuvre has four phases. In the first phase, there is a transitory rise in blood pressure as the raised intrathoracic pressure is transmitted to the periphery. During the second phase, the raised intrathoracic pressure reduces venous return and leads to a reduction in stroke volume and systemic arterial pressure, thus invoking an increase in heart rate mediated via baroreceptors. The third phase, which occurs immediately after release of strain, is characterized by a further fall in blood pressure as the reduced intrathoracic pressure is transmitted to the peripheral circulation. Finally, in the fourth phase, arterial pressure rises to higher than control levels with an associated reflex bradycardia due to an increased stroke volume resulting from dammed-up blood rushing into the heart.

Performance by the patient of a Valsalva manoeuvre during auscultation may aid clinical diagnosis. Murmurs arising from the aortic, pulmonary, tricuspid and mitral valves become diminished during the phase of strain, but murmurs originating in the ventricular outflow tracts due to hypertrophic cardiomyopathy become louder as the ventricular volume is diminished due to reduced venous return leading to increased outflow obstruction. The Valsalva manoeuvre may produce a 'square-wave' response in patients with left ventricular disease in which the first and third phases are maintained but the second and fourth phases are lost. This is because, in these subjects, the ventricle is operating on the flat upper portion of the ventricular filling curve. A reduction or increase in venous return, therefore, has little or no effect on stroke volume.

Valsalva's sinus
(Antonio Maria Valsalva, Italian anatomist and physician, 1666–1723)
see *Aortic sinus*

Valve area
The cross-sectional area of the heart valves which may be calculated using Gorlin formula. See also *Gorlin formula*

Valve, arterial
see *Arterial valve*

Valve of coronary sinus
see *Thebesian valve*

Valve of inferior caval vein
see *Eustachian valve*

Valve of Vieussens
(Raymond de Vieussens, French anatomist, 1641–1715)
It is a feature of veins within the heart, as with all veins, that they are provided with a series of simple valves which prevent flow of blood against the stream. One of the valves of the great cardiac

vein, which accompanies the anterior interventricular artery, is relatively well formed and constant, being formed at the point where the vein becomes continuous with the coronary sinus at the obtuse margin of the left ventricle. This valve is named eponymously for Vieussens.

Valves

The valves within the heart and circulation are important structures controlling the flow of blood and opening and closing passively in response to the mechanics of the cardiac cycle. The most important valves are found at the atrioventricular and ventriculoarterial junctions – the atrioventricular and arterial valves respectively. Diseases of these valves are the cause of many of the problems confronting the cardiologist. Valves are also found at the mouths of the inferior caval vein and the coronary sinus (so-called venous valves), while other venous valves are found within the lumens of the cardiac veins themselves. Nowadays, many patients also have artificial valves of varying designs inserted within the heart. Details of these various valves, both natural and artificial, are given at the appropriate point within the dictionary.

Valves, artificial

see *Artificial valves*

Valves, atrioventricular

see *Atrioventricular valves*

Valvoplasty, balloon

see *Balloon valvoplasty*

Valvotomy

Valvotomy is the surgical division of pathological fusion of the commissures of the atrioventricular or arterial valves. The operation is used to reduce stenosis of the valves and may be performed as either an open or a closed procedure. When performed as a closed procedure, the operation is often conducted using a mechanical dilator introduced transatrially. When carried out in open fashion, however, the operation is performed under direct surgical vision and, therefore, requires formal cardiopulmonary bypass. The procedure is an alternative to replacement of the afflicted valve and, normally, is confined to use in less severely diseased and less calcified valves.

Variant angina

This term refers to angina caused by transient reduction of supply of oxygen to the myocardium as a consequence of coronary arterial vasoconstriction. The coronary arterial bed is richly innervated and episodes of intense coronary vasoconstriction may provoke angina in subjects with normal coronary arteries. The electrocardiogram is then characteristic, showing elevation of the ST segment. This is referred to as Prinzmetal (or variant) angina. See *Prinzmetal angina*

Vascular rings

In the normal individual, the aortic arch is a unilateral structure, found in the left half of the thorax. During development, however, this arch, with the brachiocephalic arteries, the pulmonary arteries and the arterial duct, develop from a bilaterally symmetrical system of aortic arches. The bilateral pattern can persist in various forms in postnatal life, producing an arrangement of arterial trunks encircling the tracheoesophageal pedicle (Figure 198). The overall group of malformations in which vascular structures encircle and enclose the oesophagus are known as vascular rings. The simplest example is retroesophageal origin of one subclavian artery while the rarest is a complete double aortic arch. Not all produce difficulties in swallowing (dysphagia lusoria) but many do. When identified, the ring must be divided surgically.

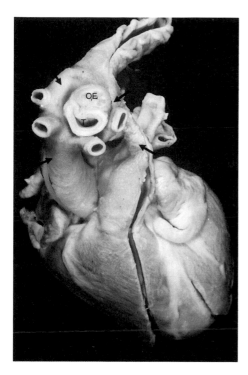

Figure 198. Vascular rings. This illustration shows a double aortic arch (arrowed) surrounding the tracheo-oesophageal pedicle. (T – trachea; OE – oesophagus)

Vascular sling

The term vascular sling describes the rare malformation in which the left pulmonary artery arises anomalously from the right pulmonary artery, running between the trachea and oesophagus to reach the hilum of the left lung. It is often associated with abnormal formation of the tracheobronchial cartilage rings as complete circular structures. Treatment is surgical, with division of the sling and reattachment of the left pulmonary artery.

Vasodilator therapy

The phrase vasodilator therapy is a blanket term used to describe drug treatment in which cardiac performance is enhanced by modulation of the peripheral circulation rather than by a direct action on the heart itself. Vasodilator drugs can conveniently be placed into two main groups. Drugs such as the nitrates dilate predominantly the capacitance vessels and their action is to decrease preload. They thus reduce filling pressure of the ventricles which may lead to an improvement in the symptoms associated with raised pulmonary or systemic venous pressures. In contrast, drugs such as hydralazine dilate predominantly the arterial vessels. They thus reduce the load against which the heart is working (afterload), leading to enhanced systolic emptying of the ventricular cavities, increased stroke volume, and reduced ventricular wall tension and myocardial consumption of oxygen. The concept of vasodilator therapy as treatment for patients with acute or chronic heart failure has enjoyed a tremendous vogue during the past 15 years. Regrettably, with two notable exceptions, the haemodynamic benefits conferred in patients with heart failure do not seem to be translated into either long-term symptomatic improvement or increased survival. The exceptions are referred to in the Consensus Study of Enalapril and the Veterans Administration Study of Hydralazine and Isorbide dinitrate.

Vasomotor syncope

see *Syncope*

Vaughan Williams classification.

This classification of antiarrhythmic drugs is based on the cellular electrophysiological properties of the drug as seen on the action potential of cardiac cells. There are four classes. In the first, (Class I), the drugs depress the upstroke velocity of the action potential. Drugs in first class are local anaesthetic agents, as typified by lignocaine, quinidine disopyramide and flecainide. The second class, (Class II),

is made up of the beta blockers. The
third class, (Class III), consists of those
antiarrhythmic drugs which prolong the
action potential duration. Amiodarone is
the archetype of this class, but typical
action is also shown by the beta blocker,
sotalol. The fourth class, (Class IV),
consists of antiarrhythmic drugs which
antagonize the actions of calcium, such
as verapamil and diltiazem.

The classification has short comings
in that it offers no place for the
commonest antiarrhythmic agent,
digoxin. Furthermore, it has little direct
extrapolation to patients with given
arrhythmias, since one arrhythmia of
a certain type will respond to drugs of
several classes.

Vector diagram
Diagrams of this type represent the
direction and magnitude of electromotive
forces of the heart, being based on
analysis of standard electrocardiographic
recordings.

Vectorcardiography
This technique is the registration of
the time course of the magnitude and
direction of cardiac electrical signals.
The cardiac vector is measured at
intervals (such as 2.5 ms) and can
then be plotted in each of the 3 planes
derived from 3 leads (transverse – X
lead, frontal – Y lead, and sagittal – Z
lead). The vectorcardiogram differs from
the standard electrocardiogram only
in its ability to display the direction of
the cardiac force with time. Because
this particular attribute fails to add
further clinical information, and because
vectorcardiography is more complex, the
technique is not widely used.

Vein graft
see *Saphenous vein graft*

Vein of Galen fistula
(Claudius Galen, Greek physician,
c.129–199 A.D.)

The commonest systemic arteriovenous
fistula is found within the head, where
the run-off to the venous side produces
marked dilatation of the transverse
sinuses and the vein of Galen. The entity,
therefore, is described as a fistula of the
vein of Galen. It presents with cardiac
failure. See also *Systemic arteriovenous
fistula*

Vein of Marshall
(John Marshall, English anatomist,
1818–1891)

During development of the heart, large
venous channels connect both the right
and left sides of the head and upper
body to the growing atria. With normal
development, the left side of these
channels regresses, persisting only as
the coronary sinus. Its original position
across the back of the left atrium is
marked by the oblique vein, named
after Marshall. The obliterated portion is
represented by the ligament of Marshall.
Should the channel persist, it is described
as the left superior caval vein. See also
Persistent left superior caval vein

Vena cava
The two great cardiac veins (superior
and inferior) were named by ancient
anatomists as the hollow veins (cava
= hollow). Retention of these Latin
words in the present day cardiological
literature leads to numerous solecisms.
For example, what is the plural of 'vena
cava', and how should the phrase be used
adjectivally? Not in terms of 'vena caval',
since flow, for example, is venous rather
than hollow. Syntax is greatly improved
by describing caval veins rather than
'vena cava'.

Vena cava syndrome
see *Superior caval venous obstruction*

Veno-occlusive disease
This rare disease of unknown aetiology
affects principally children and young
adults. It is characterized by progressive

fibrotic obstruction of both the large and small pulmonary veins. The diagnosis is confirmed by biopsy which, on histological examination, shows intimal fibrosis with organized thrombus obstructing the venous channels. The pulmonary arterial pressure is normally greatly elevated in patients with the condition, but the chest x-ray (unlike other causes of severe pulmonary hypertension such as pulmonary thromboembolic disease, primary pulmonary hypertension or Eisenmenger's syndrome) shows evidence of pulmonary venous congestion with oedema and Kerley lines. The progress of the disease is normally remorseless, although some benefit has now been reported from immunosuppressive therapy. Heart-lung transplantation is the only realistic hope for afflicted subjects.

Venous duct

(*also known as* Ductus venosus) During intrauterine development, the richly oxygenated blood for the circulation within the fetus is carried from the placenta in the umbilical vein. A large channel, the venous duct, joins this vein to the terminal part of the inferior caval vein so that the blood enters the right atrium immediately opposite the oval foramen. The duct closes immediately after birth in a fashion comparable to closure of the arterial duct. This particular part of the fetal circulation tends to be less well-recognized than does the arterial duct. See also *Fetal circulation*

Venous hum

see *Cervical venous hum*

Venous pressure

see *Central venous pressure*

Venous sinus

see *Sinus venosus*

Venous thrombosis

Venous thrombosis occurs when clots of blood are formed within the lumen of the systemic veins. By far the most common site of formation of thrombus is in the deep veins of the leg and pelvis, but thrombosis may occur in any vein, including the hepatic vein (Budd-Chiari syndrome), renal veins, retinal veins, or in the superior or inferior caval veins. Virchow's triad are three factors which, if present, make formation of thrombus more likely. These are, first, evidence of stagnation or slowing of venous flow. This may occur in patients with low cardiac output due to heart disease, or in subjects whose limbs are kept immobile, as following orthopaedic surgery or during long haul airflights. The second factor is damage to the vessel wall. This may be due to an inflammatory disease process, invasion of the vessel wall by tumour, the consequence of irradiation, or may be produced iatrogenically as, for example, during central venous cannulation, insertion of pacemakers or during cardiac catheterization. The third factor is changes in the coagulability of blood, such as is found in congenital deficiency of antithrombin III. Venous thrombosis may lead to local complications, such as oedema, but the principal and most feared problem is pulmonary embolism. Alternatively, if there is the capacity for right-to-left shunting, there may be paradoxical embolism.

Venous ventricle

The use of this term stems from the time when there was disagreement concerning the most appropriate way of describing the chambers in congenitally malformed hearts with abnormal segmental interconnexions. Thus, in the patient with a discordant atrioventricular connexion, the right atrium, receiving the systemic venous return, is inappropriately connected to the morphologically left ventricle. This left ventricle, therefore,

Venous ventricle

pumps the systemic venous return and, in
some descriptions, is termed the venous
ventricle. If, however, the chamber
connexions are described in terms of
their morphology, the haemodynamic
arrangement produced is self evident,
and there is no need for relatively non-
specific terms like venous or arterial
ventricle.

Ventilation-perfusion abnormality
see *Lung scan*

Ventricle
The ventricular mass of the heart
extends from the atrioventricular
to the ventriculoarterial junctions.
Chambers within this mass are described
as ventricles. Almost always there
are two such chambers which, in
the normally structured heart, each
possess inlet, apical trabecular and
outlet components. It is the apical
trabecular part which is the most
constant component, and the pattern
of the septal surface together with the
trabeculations always permits ventricles
to be distinguished as morphologically
right and morphologically left, even when
one of the ventricles may not possess
all its component parts, as often occurs
when the heart is congenitally malformed
(Figure 199). Very rarely, the ventricular
mass may be made up of a solitary
ventricle, which then has very coarse
apical trabeculations which are of neither
right nor left pattern. Such a ventricle is
said to be morphologically indeterminate.

Ventricular aneurysm
see *Aneurysm*

Ventricular assist pumping
see *Artificial heart: Left ventricular
assist device: Total artificial heart*

Ventricular bigeminy
see *Bigeminy*

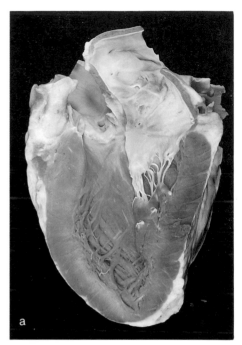

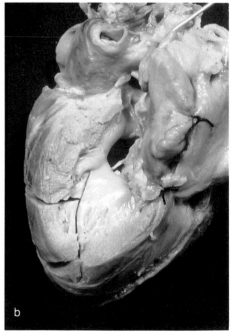

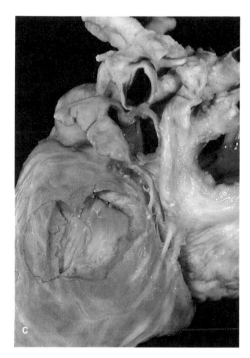

Figure 199. Ventricle. These illustrations show that the ventricle (in this case the left ventricle) is recognizable on the basis of its septal morphology and apical trabecular pattern when it is normally constructed (a) and also when it lacks an inlet component (b) or both inlet and outlet components (c).

Ventricular compliance
see *Compliance: Diastolic function*

Ventricular demand pacemakers
see *Pacemakers*

Ventricular dysfunction
This overall term refers to abnormal function of the ventricles due to any cause, be it ischaemic heart disease, cardiomyopathic processes or associated valvar heart disease.

Ventricular fibrillation
This term describes the total disorganization of the electrical

activity of the ventricles, during which ventricular myocardial cells, or groups of cells, depolarize chaotically (Figure 200).

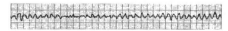

Figure 200. Ventricular fibrillation. This electrocardiographic lead shows the chaotic and disorganized electrical activity of the ventricles characteristic of ventricular fibrillation.

Effective ventricular contractions cease and, unless the arrhythmia is corrected by defibrillation or the circulation is supported by mechanical means, death follows within 3-5 minutes. Support to circumvent the arrhythmia may either be cardiopulmonary resuscitaton or cardiopulmonary bypass, and is needed until defibrillation is available. During fibrillation, the surface electrocardiogram shows irregular continuous waveforms of varying contour and amplitude. Ventricular fibrillation may occur as a primary disturbance of rhythm without prior arrhythmia or haemodynamic collapse. It may be the consequence of a predisposing disturbance of rhythm such as ventricular tachycardia, or it may result from sudden loss of cardiac output. In acute myocardial infarction, where ventricular fibrillation occurs without antecedent ventricular tachycardia or haemodynamic instability, fibrillation is regarded as primary. It then has an excellent prognosis once the arrhythmia has been corrected. In contrast, when fibrillation occurs in the context of shock, it is considered secondary and indicates a dire prognosis. Ventricular fibrillation may occur in all forms of heart disease but is seen most commonly in the context of coronary arterial disease. It may also occur as a consequence of therapy, particularly following use of antiarrhythmic drugs or

Ventricular fibrillation

electrical treatment, as well as occurring with electrocution. The majority of those with out-of-hospital sudden cardiac death have ventricular fibrillation, usually the consequence of initially rapid ventricular tachycardia. Defibrillation must be instituted immediately by transthoracic shock using direct current, usually requiring 200-400 joules.

Ventricular flutter
This abnormal rhythm is the consequence of organized and rapid ventricular depolarizations which arises from the ventricles and which, on the surface electrocardiogram, produce a sinusoidal pattern of high amplitude. The rate is usually in the range of 180 – 300 beats per minute. The arrhythmia differs from ventricular tachycardia in that there is not clear onset or offset relative to the QRS complexes. There is usually no effective cardiac output, and the rhythm may quickly degenerate into ventricular fibrillation. The causes and treatment are as for ventricular fibrillation.

Ventricular function
Ventricular function refers to those mechanical events occurring in the ventricular myocardium following electrical depolarization. In broad terms, ventricular function may be divided into systolic and diastolic events. Systolic events occur following the onset of ventricular contraction, this coinciding with the peak of the R wave of the electrocardiogram. There is initially a rapid rise in interventricular pressure which closes the mitral and tricuspid valves. After closure of the atrioventricular valves, there is a rapid rise of pressure in the ventricles prior to opening of the arterial valves. During this stage, there may be changes in the shape of the ventricle but no change in volume. This phase is referred to as the isovolumic period. When the ventricular pressure exceeds that in the arterial trunks, the arterial valves

open and ventricular ejection occurs. The highest rate of flow occurs early in systole as pressures rise in the aorta and pulmonary trunk. As the strength of ventricular contraction declines, the aortic and pulmonary valves close and the diastolic phase follows. Diastolic function is described in detail elsewhere in this dictionary. See also *Myocardial function*

Ventricular fusion beat
This describes ventricular depolarization produced by two independent depolarizing wavefronts which merge together to produce a QRS complex representing fusion between the patterns produced by each individual wavefront. The contribution from each of the wavefronts, and therefore the degree of fusion, is dependent on the timing of each impulse. The commonest pattern of ventricular fusion beat is seen when an impulse originating in the ventricles fuses with a supraventricular conducted impulse. This variant is one hallmark of ventricular tachycardia.

Ventricular loop
During development of the heart, the primordium of the ventricular component is initially a straight tube connecting the proximal atrial to the distal arterial segments. With growth, the tube bends so that the arterial pole comes to lie in front of the developing atria. This process of bending produces the ventricular loop from which, eventually, are derived the definitive right and left ventricles. (Figure 201)

Ventricular mapping
This is the technique of recording multiple local electrograms from the ventricular myocardium to produce a map of ventricular excitation. Local electrograms can be recorded individually in sequential fashion or from multiple points simultaneously. The map can be created from epicardial,

endocardial or transmyocardial recordings. The map can be produced during normal rhythm, to produce a map of normal depolarization, or during an arrhythmia in order to identify the origin of abnormal formation of impulses.

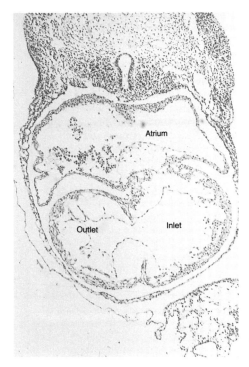

Figure 201. Ventricular loop. This micrograph of a human embryo during early development shows the inlet and outlet components of the ventricular loop.

Ventricular mass

This term describes the middle segment of the heart when analysed in terms of congenital cardiac malformations. The mass extends from the atrioventricular to the ventriculoarterial junctions.

Ventricular pacing

In this procedure, depolarization of the ventricles is produced as a result of an electrical stimulus delivered via an electrode in contact with the pericardial or endocardial surface of the myocardium. Ventricular pacing may be temporary or permanent. Generally, it is performed in order to support the cardiac rate when the spontaneous rhythm is too slow, as, for example, in complete heart block. Ventricular pacing may also be used diagnostically during electrophysiological study to determine the nature of various tachyarrhythmias. It may be employed therapeutically for the termination of both supraventricular and ventricular tachycardia. See *Pacemakers*

Ventricular pressure wave

These are the waveforms recorded in the left or right ventricles during the cardiac cycle. They have a characteristic morphology. Shortly after the QRS complex of the electrocardiogram, the ventricular pressure rapidly rises and exceeds atrial pressure to cause closure of the atrioventricular valves. Some 60 – 80 ms later, the ventricular pressure exceeds arterial pressure and promotes the opening of the arterial valves. The period between closure of the atrioventricular valves and opening of the arterial valves is known as the period of isovolumic contraction.

After opening of the arterial valves, blood is ejected from the ventricle and the pressure levels out, falling towards the end of ejection. The arterial pressure exceeds ventricular pressure during the second half of ejection, but blood flow continues because of the momentum imparted to it during the first half of ejection.

At the end of ejection, the leaflets of the arterial valves close and ventricular pressure falls in an exponential fashion until it is lower than atrial pressure. At this time, the leaflets of the atrioventricular valves open and ventricular filling begins.

The period between closure of the arterial valves and opening of the atrioventricular valves is known as

the period of isovolumic relaxation.
After atrioventricular valvar opening,
ventricular pressure continues to fall
despite the fact that volume is increasing.
This is because relaxation at this time
is an active process. Eventually, the
ventricular pressure reaches a nadir and
begins to rise in a curvilinear fashion,
the slope of ascent being determined
by the mechanical properties of the
myocardium. At the end of this period
of passive filling, or diastasis, atrial
contraction occurs, leading to an increase
in ventricular pressure termed the A
wave. The cycle then begins again.

Ventricular septal defect

A deficiency of the ventricular septum,
permitting an interatrial communication,
is by far the commonest type of
congenital cardiac malformation, making
up nearly one-third of the lesions seen
in liveborn infants. Often a ventricular
septal defect is an integral part of other
anomalies, such as tricuspid atresia,
double inlet or outlet ventricle, and
common arterial trunk. The defect can
also occur as a complicating lesion, as
in complete or congenitally corrected
transposition. When used as 'ventricular
septal defect', however, the term usually
describes the isolated lesion in the
patient with an otherwise normally
structured heart and in the absence of
major complicating lesions. It was Roger
who, as long ago as 1879, described
how such isolated defects produced
a typical murmur at auscultation and
could be consistent with prolonged life
and good health. In anatomic terms, the
defects can be found in various parts of
the septum, but are divided into three
major groups. The majority are found
within the inner curvature of the heart,
and abut directly on the central fibrous
body (continuity between the leaflets of
the tricuspid, aortic and mitral valves).
These defects are, nowadays, usually
described as being perimembranous,
since they are adjacent to the area

of the membranous septum, which
forms part of their perimeter. The rarer
forms of defect are either embedded
within the substance of the septum
(muscular defects) or else roofed by
fibrous continuity between the leaflets
of the aortic and pulmonary valves
(doubly committed and juxta-arterial
defects). The presence of a ventricular
septal defect is rarely, if ever, detected
at birth. This is because the high level
of pulmonary resistance found in the
first few weeks of postnatal life limits
shunting across the defect. Most large
defects, therefore, come to be noticed
in the second month of life, usually
with difficulty in feeding and failure to
thrive. Smaller, restrictive, defects may
be discovered at any age through their
characteristic murmur. The murmur is
pansystolic and is localized to the second
and third left intercostal spaces. Although
electrocardiographic, radiographic and
angiographic findings are of value in
diagnosis, most information nowadays
is obtained from cross-sectional
echocardiography. This technique
identifies the site and nature of the
defect, and use of Doppler and colour-
flow facilities permits estimations of
flow across the defect to be made, the
chance of spontaneous closure and the
level of right ventricular pressure. It is
these three features which determine
the natural history of the lesion. Many
defects are small and restrictive, and
do not increase in size, rather showing a
tendency to close spontaneously. Patients
with these small defects can lead normal
lives, but should receive prophylactic
therapy against endocarditis during
procedures such as dental therapy. Those
with large and unrestrictive defects
present during infancy and need surgical
treatment, which is now carried out
during infancy with a success rate of 95%
or more. Some complicated defects may
require palliation initially, by banding of
the pulmonary trunk, but these are in
a small minority. In those patients with

defects of intermediate size, the crucial feature is the state of the pulmonary vasculature, since there is always the risk of developing irreversible vascular disease. Nowadays, therefore, whenever the picture is equivocal, it is usual to err on the side of surgical closure. The postoperative status is generally excellent after successful closure, although many recommend antibiotic prophylaxis during dental treatment and so on.

Ventricular septal rupture

Ventricular septal rupture is a rare and life threatening complication of acute myocardial infarction. The characteristic clinical picture is that of a patient who has been recovering well from an episode of infarction who suddenly deteriorates with features of hypotension and right heart failure, deterioration which is associated with the development of a new pansystolic murmur normally loudest at the left sternal edge and often accompanied by a palpable thrill. The diagnosis is most easily confirmed by the insertion of a catheter into the right heart which identifies a step-up in saturation of oxygen within blood sampled at ventricular level due to the left-to-right shunting across the ruptured septum. Cross-sectional echocardiography, Doppler ultrasound and conventional left ventricular cineangiography may also be useful if the diagnosis is in doubt. Early surgical repair of the rupture is advisable, even though the immediate operative mortality is high. Most series report a survival rate of only 40% to 50% at one year. Ventricular septal rupture is associated with a worse prognosis when seen in the context of inferior infarction than for rupture in the context of anterior infarction. See also *Myocardial rupture*

Ventricular tachycardia

This abnormal rhythm is the consequence of formation of impulses within the specialized conducting tissue distal to

the bifurcation of the atrioventricular bundle, in the ventricular myocardium or in a combination of both tissues. The rate may be in the range of 100 – 250 beats per minute. It is characterized on the electrocardiogram by broad QRS complexes which exceed 120 ms in duration. The RR intervals may be regular or irregular. Atrial activity may be independent, as in atrioventricular dissocation, in which case the diagnosis of ventricular tachycardia will be certain. There may, however, be retrograde atrial depolarization, in which case differentiation from supraventricular tachycardia associated with aberrant conduction will require other diagnostic information. Fusion (or capture) beats are diagnostic of ventricular tachycardia (Figure 202). Other features that support the diagnosis of ventricular tachycardia, but are not diagnostic, are a pattern, the first R wave being taller than the second.

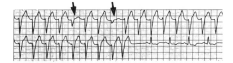

Figure 202. Ventricular tachycardia with fusion beat. This continuous rhythm strip shows ventricular tachycardia and spontaneous conversion to sinus rhythm. During ventricular tachycardia, there is atrioventricular dissociation. When a sinus discharge is conducted and depolarizes part of the ventricles at the same time as an ectopic depolarization, there is fusion of depolarization and the QRS complex is intermediate in form between a beat (arrowed) conducted from the sinus node and a depolarization resulting entirely from the tachycardia.

It is customary to describe the QRS complexes during ventricular tachycardia as having a right or left 'bundle branch block' configuration based on the appearance of the QRS complex in lead V1. Differentiation of ventricular from supraventricular tachycardia is essential as the treatment of the two is usually quite different. Treatment suitable for supraventricular tachycardia may be lethal if given erroneously to the patient with ventricular tachycardia. Ventricular tachycardia can be characterized into patterns on the basis of the QRS contour. The arrhythmia may be *monomorphic* with unchanging QRS complexes. When it shows randomly changing complexes it is said to be *polymorphic*. Repetitive changes are characteristic of *torsade*, while alternate QRS axes are the criteria for *bidirectional* morphology. Ventricular tachycardia may be sustained or non-sustained, the latter being defined arbitrarily as lasting less than 30 seconds, or requiring termination because of haemodynamic collapse. An electrophysiological study may be required to differentiate ventricular from supraventricular tachycardia. Electrophysiological study may also be employed to induce sustained ventricular tachycardia and guide antiarrhythmic therapy.

Ventricular tachycardia complicates all forms of heart disease, particularly chronic ischaemic heart disease. For this reason, it is most common in middle age but may be seen at all ages. It may also occur in the absence of demonstrable heart disease. While the presence of ventricular tachycardia may always imply an adverse prognosis, the risk to the patient is predominantly determined by the presence and severity of the underlying cardiac disease.

During ventricular tachycardia, the symptoms and haemodynamic status will depend upon the ventricular rate, the duration of tachycardia, and the extent of associated heart disease but will vary from being asymptomatic to producing immediate haemodynamic collapse. In patients resuscitated from sudden cardiac death, ventricular tachycardia is the most frequently provokable arrhythmia and, in ambulatory recordings of patients during sudden cardiac death, ventricular tachycardia is the usual initial arrhythmia which degenerates into ventricular fibrillation.

Acute treatment of sustained ventricular tachycardia should be with drugs, pacing or cardioversion using direct current, thumpversion may be effective. Prevention of recurrences requires correction of the provoking factors, such as electrolyte disturbance, drug toxicity, or associated heart disease. Long term treatment, if required, will be with drugs, surgery or implantation of a cardioverter/defibrillator.

Ventricular topology

The ventricular mass of the heart almost always, even when the heart is grossly malformed, contains two ventricles, one of right and the other of left morphology. There are only two ways in which the morphologically right and left ventricles can be related one to the other. The usual pattern is that seen in normal persons, and in most of those with congenital malformations. The other pattern is a mirror-image variant, seen exceedingly rarely in those who have complete mirror-image arrangement of the organs (situs inversus) but more frequently (although rare in the overall context) in those who have anomalies such as congenitally corrected transposition. The two topological patterns of ventricular arrangement are described in terms of the way the palmar surface of the observer's right hand can, figuratively speaking, be laid on the septal surface of the morphologically right ventricle such that the thumb goes into the inlet and the fingers into the outlet. These two variants are described as right hand and left hand patterns, respectively.

Ventriculoarterial concordance

A concordant ventriculoarterial connexion, often described in terms of ventriculoarterial concordance, exists when the aorta is connected to the morphologically left ventricle or its rudiment and the pulmonary trunk is connected to the morphologically right ventricle or its rudiment.

Ventriculoarterial connexions

The connexion of the arterial trunks to the ventricular mass is the most important of the variable features of the ventriculoarterial junction which may be found in congenitally malformed hearts. The other features, requiring separate description when abnormal, are the morphology of the arterial valves, the arrangement of the infundibular musculature and the relationships of the arterial trunks. In terms of the connexions, there are four basic patterns. A concordant ventriculoarterial connexion exists when the arterial trunks arise from their appropriate ventricles, whereas origin of the trunks from morphologically inappropriate ventricles is described in terms of a discordant connexion. Double outlet connexion is defined when both arterial trunks are connected to the same ventricle, which may be of right, left or indeterminate morphology. Hearts with overriding arterial valves are dealt with by allocating the overriding arterial trunk to the ventricle supporting the greater part of its circumference. The fourth type of connexion is single outlet of the heart. This can itself be found in four patterns. A common arterial trunk is most frequent. The other patterns are a solitary pulmonary trunk with aortic atresia, a solitary aortic trunk with pulmonary atresia or a solitary arterial trunk. These latter variants are defined at the appropriate point of the dictionary.

Ventriculoarterial discordance

The arrangement in congenitally malformed hearts in which the arterial trunks arise from morphologically inappropriate ventricles (aorta from right ventricle and pulmonary trunk from left ventricle) is best described as a discordant ventriculoarterial connexion, although often described simply as ventriculoarterial discordance.

Ventriculoarterial junction

The ventriculoarterial junction is the area of the heart where the arterial trunks are attached to the ventricular mass. The anatomic arrangement is complicated by the fact that, although the walls of the arterial trunks are attached to their supporting ventricles in annular fashion, the leaflets of the arterial valves are attached across this anatomic ventriculoarterial junction in semilunar fashion (Figure 203). This discordance between the anatomic and haemodynamic junctions means that, in terms of physiologic pressures, a small part of the arterial wall at the apex of each valvar commissure is part of the ventricular outflow tract, while small components of the ventricular walls are incorporated in the bases of the three arterial sinuses of Valsalva.

Figure 203. Ventriculoarterial junction. This dissection of the pulmonary valve, made by removing the leaflets, shows how the leaflets are attached in semilunar fashion across the circular anatomic ventriculoarterial junction.

Ventriculoarterial junction

The ventriculoarterial junction is also important in congenitally malformed hearts, since the anatomic arrangement can be anomalous in several fashions. In those with abnormal ventriculoarterial junctions, attention must be focussed separately on the precise connexion of the arterial trunks to the ventricular mass; the morphology of the leaflets of the arterial valves guarding the junction; the extent of the infundibular musculature supporting the arterial trunks; and the relationships of the arterial trunks to each other as they exit from the ventricular mass.

Ventriculography

This blanket term is used to describe any method of imaging the ventricular cavities. By far the most common ventriculographic method is the injection of radiopaque dyes into the ventricular cavities, the images being recorded using an image intensifier and a 35 mm cinecamera. Ventriculograms may also be recorded using radionuclide techniques. Calibrated ventriculograms allow measurements of ventricular dimensions, volume and shape. Atrioventricular valvar regurgitation can be detected and its severity quantified. The pattern of wall motion throughout the cardiac cycle can be observed. Left ventricular cineangiograms are conventionally recorded with the imaging camera in the right or left anterior oblique projections, although selected projections may be best for identification of abnormal features found in patients with congenitally malformed hearts. Right ventricular cineangiograms are normally recorded in the anteroposterior and/or true lateral projections.

Ventriculo-infundibular fold

During development of the heart, the ventricular part bends upon itself to produce the ventricular loop, which then has inner and outer curvatures. The inner curvature separates the sites of the developing atrioventricular and arterial valves. With completion of development, this inner curve persists in the right ventricle as the muscular roof of the ventricle between the pulmonary and tricuspid valves. This part of the ventricular musculature is described as the ventriculo-infundibular fold. Normally, the inner curvature within the left ventricle becomes attenuated so that the leaflets of the aortic and mitral valves are in fibrous continuity. In malformed hearts, however, musculature can be found in the inner curvature between the aortic and both atrioventricular valves. This structure is also part of the ventriculo infundibular fold.

Ventriculotomy

Any incision into a ventricle is described in surgical terms as a ventriculotomy.

Venturi effect

(G.B. Venturi, Italian physician, 1746-1822)
This is an effect produced when blood is driven from a high-pressure source (the left ventricle) through an orifice (the nearly closed but regurgitant mitral valve) into a low-pressure sink (the atrium).

Verapamil

Verapamil is a calcium antagonist agent which inhibits the inward movement of calcium in cardiac cells, the cells of the atrioventricular penetrating bundle, and systemic and coronary arterial smooth muscle cells. Administration of verapamil reduces the force of cardiac contraction, prolongs atrioventricular conduction and dilates systemic and coronary arteries. These various properties of the drug make it useful in a number of clinical situations:
by lowering peripheral resistance, it is an effective antihypertensive agent;
as an effective antianginal agent presumably because it reduces myocardial contraction as a consequence

of reduced heart rate and contractility
and lowered systemic vascular resistance;
as a potent antiarrhythmic agent, which
is widely employed in the suppression
of supraventricular and fascicular
tachycardias.

Verapamil should be administered with
caution to subjects with impaired left
ventricular function in whom it may
precipitate heart failure, and to subjects
receiving concomitant therapy with beta-
adrenergic antagonist agents in whom it
may provoke bradycardias or complete
heart block.

Very low density lipoproteins
see *Lipoproteins*

Visceral heterotaxy
It is well recognized that the most
complex congenitally malformed
hearts are often found in syndromes
characterized by an abnormal
arrangement of the organs within the
remainder of the body. The overall
group of patients thus afflicted is
usually described in terms of visceral
heterotaxy. The abdominal organs in
these syndromes tend to show lack
of the expected symmetry, with a
midline liver, a malrotated gut and either
absence of the spleen or presence of
multiple spleens. In terms of the thoracic
organs, however, including the atrial
appendages, there is evidence of marked
symmetry, and visceral heterotaxy can
be divided into groups characterized
by left and right isomerism, the right-
sided structures being isomers of their
left-sided counterparts. Diagnosis of
the complex cardiac malformations,
therefore, is best approached from
the stance of isomerism of the atrial
appendages, thus setting the scene for
subsequent sequential segmental analysis.
Although the syndromes are often
described also in terms of ambiguous
situs, and while the abdominal organs
show no order in their arrangement, the
thoracic organs are isomeric rather than

ambiguous. See also *Asplenia: Atrial
isomerism: Polysplenia*

Volume
This is the space occupied by any form
of matter. It is usually expressed in cubic
millimetres, cubic centimetres, litres and
so on.

W – Z

Warfarin
see *Anticoagulant drugs*

Water hammer pulse
This is a term used by old fashioned clinicians to describe a rapidly rising brisk arterial pulse. A water hammer was a Victorian toy consisting of a tube containing a volume of water and a vacuum. When the tube was inverted the water, unopposed by the vacuum, drops like a stone producing a noise similar to that of a hammer and a tactile sensation reputed to be similar to the character of the pulse found in severe aortic regurgitation.

Waterston's groove
(David Waterston, British anatomist, twentieth century)
This deep groove marks the external site of the interatrial septum. Its extent is often marked by the epicardium bridging across from the right pulmonary veins to the venous sinus of the right atrium. Sharp dissection of this area, however, reveals that the superior rim of the oval fossa is the infolded atrial wall. It is this infolding which is Waterston's groove. It provides excellent access to the left atrium during surgical procedures.

Waterston shunt
(David James Waterston, English paediatric surgeon, born 1910)
This systemic-to-pulmonary shunt is constructed by making small openings in the back wall of the aorta and the front of the right pulmonary artery and anastomosing the two around the openings. It is difficult to construct and, although offering excellent palliation in skilled hands, has tended to be superseded by shunts constructed by placing a prosthetic tube between the subclavian and pulmonary arteries (modified Blalock-Taussig shunts).

Wedge pressure
This is the pressure recorded when a catheter has been passed through the pulmonary arterial system as far as it will go, so that it is pressed tightly against the arteriolar capillary junction. At this point, the recorded pressure reflects the pressure in the pulmonary venous system and is, therefore, an indirect measure of left atrial pressure.

Wenckebach block
(Karel Frederik Wenckebach, Dutch physician, 1864-1940)
This variant of second degree block is characterized by a progressive increase in the conduction time through conduction tissue until an impulse is blocked. Also known as type I second degree block and Mobitz I block, it is most commonly seen with dysfunction of the atrioventricular node. See also *Heart block*

Whipple's disease
(George Hoyt Whipple, U.S. pathologist, born 1878)
see *Intestinal lipodystrophy*

Williams' syndrome
This syndrome of mild to moderate mental retardation is associated with a characteristic facial appearance, with prominent orbital ridges, thick lips, large and ridged teeth and a slight squint. It is also associated with supravalvar aortic stenosis as the characteristic cardiac lesion. First described as a syndrome by Williams and his colleagues from New Zealand, it was shortly after that that the group at Great Ormond Street Hospital, London, established the association of the syndrome with idiopathic hypercalcaemia. The major pathology is at the level of the commissures of the aortic valve and, if severe, surgery is needed for its relief.

Windkessel model

Arterial vessels distend during systole to accept the volume of blood ejected by the ventricle. Then, during diastole, the arteries contract, due to recoil of the elastic elements in their walls, expelling blood into the peripheral circulation. This concept, that arteries store blood during systole and eject it during diastole, was first propounded by Stephen Hales in 1733. It was not until 1899, however, that the theory was shown mathematically by Otto Frank, who used a compliant air chamber (or Windkessel) as his model. Subsequent analysis has shown that the properties of the systemic arteries are inadequately described by this so-called Windkessel theory but that the properties of the pulmonary arterial system roughly approximate to the model.

Wolff-Parkinson-White syndrome

(Louis Wolff, U.S. cardiologist, born 1898: Sir John Parkinson, British physician, born 1885: Paul Dudley White, U.S. cardiologist, 1886-1973)
This syndrome comprises the electrocardiographic features of a short PR interval, a delta wave, widened QRS complex and a tendency to paroxysmal tachycardia. It is produced by conduction across occurring atrioventricular muscular connexions which cross the three planes between atrial and ventricular muscle masses outside the confines of the specialized atrioventricular conduction axis. This creates the potential for circus movements around the anomalous connection and the normal axis of conduction. See *Ventricular pre-excitation.*

X descent

This descent describes the falling portion of the record of central venous pressure which follows atrial systole. It is due mainly to atrial diastole and, therefore, disappears together with the a wave with the onset of atrial fibrillation.

Xamoterol

This drug is a partial agonist of cardiac B_1 adrenoceptors. When administered to patients with mild to moderate heart failure, it produces measurable haemodynamic benefits which are associated with a sustained increase in capacity for exercise and a reduction in intensity of symptoms.

Xanthelasma

These lesions of the skin are found at the medial aspects of both upper and lower eyelids. In younger patients, they may be associated with elevation of serum cholesterol but, in the elderly population, they may occur (and tend to increase with age) despite a normal level of cholesterol.

Xanthoma

This is a general term given to cholesterol rich nodules which are found either subcutaneously or over tendons in patients with hypercholesterolaemia. There are four different types:
Tuberous xanthomas are yellow subcutaneous nodules found on the extensor surfaces of the arms and legs. They are most commonly seen in subjects with type II hyperlipoproteinaemia and their presence is predictive of the development of severe coronary arterial disease often at an early age.
Tendon xanthomas are nodules which particularly involve the extensor tendons of the hands and the feet.
Eruptive xanthomas are tiny yellow nodules with an erythematous base which occur transiently. They are associated with raised serum triglyceride concentrations as are found in patients with type I hyperlipoproteinaemia.
Planar xanthomas are small xanthomas found in the palmar creases.

Xenon-133 scanning

see *Scintigraphy*

Y descent

Y descent
The Y descent is that part of the trace of central venous pressure which follows ventricular systole. The descent occurs concomitantly with opening of the tricuspid or mitral valves. It becomes prominent in right ventricular failure and constrictive pericarditis.

Y wave, slow descent
see *Central venous pressure*

Z lead
see *Electrocardiogram*

Z-lines
These characteristic lines seen on electron micrographs of cardiac and skeletal muscle cells mark the boundaries of individual sarcomeres. They are attached to the sarcolemma of the cells and it is these lines which, for the most part, produce the cross-striations of these muscles. They provide the support mechanism for the actin filaments of abutting sarcomeres. See also *Cardiac cell: Myocardial structure*